Adult
Bible Study Series

By Thomas J. Doyle

Portions of the "Study" and "Apply" sections
were written by Carl C. Fickenscher II.

Catechism Connections were written
by Arnold Schmidt.

CONCORDIA PUBLISHING HOUSE • SAINT LOUIS

Edited by Arnold Schmidt and Lorraine Groth

Scripture quotations are taken from the HOLY BIBLE, NEW INTERNATIONAL VERSION®. NIV®. Copyright © 1973, 1978, 1984 by International Bible Society. Used by permission of Zondervan Publishing House. All rights reserved.

Quotations from the Small Catechism are taken from Luther's Small Catechism with Explanation, copyright © 1986, 1991 Concordia Publishing House.

Quotation from the Large Catechism is taken from The Book of Concord, ed. Theodore Tappert, copyright © 1959 Fortress Press.

This publication may be available in braille, in large print, or on cassette tape for the visually impaired. Please allow 8 to 12 weeks for delivery. Write to the Library for the Blind, 7550 Watson Rd., St. Louis, MO 63119-4409; call toll-free 1-888-215-2455; or visit the Web site: www.blindmission.org.

Manufactured in the United States of America

1   2   3   4   5   6   7   8   9   10   13   12   11   10   09   08   07   06   05   04

Contents

Introduction

God promises to strengthen our life in Christ as we study His Word. The Our Life in Christ Adult Bible Study series provides you resources to help you study God's Word. The series gives you an opportunity to study in-depth some familiar, and possibly not-so-familiar, Bible stories.

Each of the 9 Bible study books has 13 sessions that are divided into 4 easy-to-use sections.

Gather—Section 1 of each session focuses the participant's attention on the key concept that will be discovered in the session.

Study—Section 2 explores a portion of Scripture through the use of a brief commentary and through discussion questions that help the participant study the text.

Apply—Section 3 helps the participant apply to their lives God's Law and Gospel as revealed in the scriptural account.

Send—Section 4 provides the participants with practical suggestions for taking the theme of the lesson out of the classroom and into their families.

Our Life in Christ is designed to assist both novice and expert Bible students in their study of Holy Scripture. It offers resources that will enable them to grow in their understanding of God's Word while strengthening their life in Christ.

As an added benefit, the sessions in the Our Life in Christ Adult Bible Study series follow the Scripture lessons taught in the Our Life in Christ Sunday school series. Parents will enjoy studying in-depth the Bible stories their children are studying in Sunday school. This will provide parents and children additional opportunities to

- discuss God's Word together;
- apply lesson applications to everyday situations;
- pray together; and
- engage in family activities that grow out of lesson truths.

We pray that as you study God's Word using the Our Life in Christ Adult Bible Study series, your life in Christ may be strengthened.

Adult Study Guide

World History	Dates	Biblical People
Pre-historic Era		
Neo-Sumerian	2000 B.C.	
Egypt, New Kingdom	1500 B.C.	Moses Joshua
		Ruth Samuel
Philistine Invasion	1000 B.C.	King David
Assyrian Empire	785 B.C.	
Old Testament Ends	430 B.C.	Nehemiah
		Zechariah
Romans	A.D. 27	Jesus Christ

Session 1

God Calls Moses

(Exodus 2–4)

Gather

Theme: "Why Me?"

Key Point

God forgives us for our sinful thoughts, words, and actions for Jesus' sake, and through the Gospel empowers and equips us to serve Him.

Objectives

By the power of the Holy Spirit working through God's Word, we will
1. identify Moses' objections to God's call to service;
2. explain the significance of God's description of Himself as "I AM";
3. describe God's persistence, loving assurance, and patience provided to Moses;
4. confess our denial and/or rejection of God's desire for us to serve Him and rejoice in the forgiveness Jesus won for us on the cross;
5. seek new opportunities to serve God as we are motivated and empowered by Jesus' love.

Opening

Read the First Article of the Apostles' Creed and Martin Luther's explanation responsively:

All: I believe in God, the Father Almighty, Maker of heaven and earth.

Leader: What does this mean?

Group 1: I believe that God has made me and all creatures; that He has given me my body and soul, eyes, ears, and all my members, my reason and all my senses, and still takes care of them.

Group 2: He also gives me clothing and shoes, food and drink, house and home, wife and children, land, animals, and all I have. He richly and daily provides me with all that I need to support this body and life.

Group 1: He defends me against all danger and guards and protects me from all evil.

Group 2: All this He does only out of fatherly, divine goodness and mercy, without any merit or worthiness in me. For all this it is my duty to thank and praise, serve and obey Him.

All: This is most certainly true.

Introduction

"Why me?"

1. What are some situations you have encountered that led you or someone you know to ask, "Why me?"

2. How might you demonstrate a "why me?" attitude toward opportunities to tell others about God's love in Jesus? toward opportunities to serve Him with your time, talents, and treasures?

In today's lesson God calls Moses to serve Him. Moses asks, "Why me?" and then lists reasons that God should not choose him. But God in patience promises to equip Moses and remain with him as he serves.

Study

Reading the Text

The family of Israel had come to Egypt as heroes, but things had changed! The lessons for this quarter trace God's mighty acts through which He delivered a helpless nation from slavery and brought His people safely to a land of their own. The story is more than a history lesson. It is, in fact, more than a series of Old Testament Bible narratives. For the story of Israel—the Exodus, the wilderness wandering, new life in the Promised Land—is a powerful illustration of the salvation and daily guidance God gives us through Jesus Christ.

Joseph had been ruler of all Egypt (Genesis 41). In perhaps the year 1876 B.C., he had brought his father, Israel (Jacob), his 11 brothers, and their families to Goshen, the richest part of Egypt, to escape famine (Genesis 45–46). There they had prospered, growing from a clan of some 70 persons to become a nation of more than two million (Exodus 1:1–7).

However, as the Israelite nation had grown, so had resentment among its hosts. The Egyptian ruling dynasty that had honored Joseph was conquered—first by a foreign people called the Hyksos (1720[?] B.C.), then by a new Egyptian dynasty (1567 B.C.). These rulers feared the power and sheer numbers of the Israelites (1:8–10). They enslaved them, then tried to eradicate them by ordering the Israelite midwives to kill all baby boys (1:11–21). When this plan failed, Pharaoh (probably Thutmose I) ordered that male babies be drowned in the Nile (1:22).

Here God begins His marvelous plan of deliverance (2:1–10). A boy child is born to a family of the tribe of Levi. By a special act of faith (see Hebrews 11:23), his parents defy Pharaoh's order. They prepare a basket and hide the child in it; they then set the basket adrift in the shallow water along the riverbank. (The basket was made of papyrus—dried river grass—and probably looked like a miniature version of an Egyptian papyrus sea ship.)

There the baby is discovered, perhaps by one of the most famous women of the ancient world: Hatshepsut. The daughter of Pharaoh, Hatshepsut was a strong woman who herself later ruled as Pharaoh for more than 20 years. (Egyptian religious beliefs and custom dictated that as Pharaoh she masquerade as a man!) The princess adopts the child and gives him an Egyptian royal name: Moses, a name rooted in her father's name, Pharaoh Thut*mose*. Thus, in a remarkable arrangement by God, Moses grows up with the finest training of Egyptian civilization, and yet his own Hebrew mother is paid to nurse him (2:7–10)!

Unfortunately, Moses' own grasp of God's plan was incomplete at best (see Acts 7:22–28). After rashly attempting to rally his fellow Israelites against their oppressors by killing an Egyptian, he is forced to flee (Exodus 2:11–15). At age 40, probably in the year 1486 B.C., Moses seems likely to disappear from history, living as a shepherd in the land of Midian.

Instead, after 40 more years, as Moses is tending his sheep at Mount Horeb (Mount Sinai), the Lord calls him to change history. The "angel of the Lord" who speaks from a burning bush (3:2) is none other than God Himself (3:4). (This is one of many passages in the Old Testament in which the angel or "messenger" of the Lord is probably the Son of God, long before His becoming flesh as Jesus of Nazareth.) The Lord identifies Himself with the three patriarchs all Israelites admired: "I am the God of Abraham, Isaac, and Jacob." He has seen Israel's suffering and intends to deliver His people (3:6–9).

"So now, go. I am sending *you* to Pharaoh to bring My people the Israelites out of Egypt" (3:10, emphasis added). Why me? Moses now begins two chapters of back-pedaling from God's call. But for each objection, God has a loving—and winning—answer.

Objection 1. *Moses* (to paraphrase): "I'm a nobody—why should Pharaoh listen to me?" (3:11). *God:* "I will be with you" (3:12).

Objection 2. *Moses:* "The Israelites don't even know who You are—and neither do I, really!" (3:13). *God:* I AM who I AM "This is what you are to say to the Israelites: 'I AM has sent me to you.'... This is my name forever, the name by which I am to be remembered from generation to generation" (3:14–15).

Objection 3. *Moses:* "They won't buy my story on words alone!" (4:1). *God:* "This is so that they may believe that the Lord has appeared to you ..." God gives Moses miraculous signs to perform in order to prove his claim (3:2–9).

Objection 4. *Moses:* "Lord, this job takes a persuasive orator, and everybody knows I can't speak well" (4:10). *God:* "Who gave man his mouth?… I will help you speak and teach you what to say" (4:11–12).

Objection 5. *Moses:* "Lord, I'm just too scared! Please send somebody else" (4:13). *God:* "What about your brother, Aaron the Levite? He will speak to the people for you" (4:14, 16).

Discussing the Text

1. How did God's plan for deliverance take shape even in the infancy and childhood of Moses? What does this incident reveal about God?

2. How did Moses demonstrate that his understanding of God's plan for deliverance was incomplete (see Exodus 2:11–15)? What does this incident reveal about God?

3. On the chart on the next page list each of Moses' objections to God's call to service and God's response.

Moses' Objections	God's Response

4. How did God demonstrate patience in His dealings with Moses?

Apply

"I AM with you, Moses ... I AM with My people at all times and everywhere they go." God's clear assurance to Moses and a powerful assurance for us is His name by which He has chosen to be called and praised.

The name I AM (from which comes the Hebrew, Yahweh, indicated in English translations as *"the LORD"*) expresses the limitlessness of God. He can never be fully described by saying "He is this" or "He is that." *He simply is* ... and that is that.

As a result, I AM also describes how readily present God is: "Today, as you're here, I AM here. Yesterday, when you were there, I AM there. Tomorrow, wherever you'll be, I AM." When it seemed God had forgotten His people in bondage, *He is* there, preparing their liberation. As Moses lay helpless in the river basket, *He is* there, drawing the princess to save the day. When God called Moses to stand virtually alone before Pharaoh, *He is* with His servant, with him in fact at every moment.

We, too, face struggles, fear, and pain. Work seems too difficult. Life at home is unstable. Friends are cruel. We also face challenges that might appear wholesome and productive, but are actually overwhelming. Yet every place, every day those struggles or challenges arise, God is with us. With I AM beside us, we have God's limitless help and comfort, and we are able to do anything He asks.

No wonder Jesus so often spoke of Himself as I AM: "I AM the Bread of Life" (John 6:35, emphasis added), "before Abraham was, I AM" (8:58), "I AM the Light of the World" (9:5), "I AM the Door" (10:7), "I AM the Good Shepherd," (10:11), "I AM the Resurrection and the Life" (11:25), "I AM the Way and the Truth and the Life" (14:6), "I AM the True Vine" (15:1). Jesus, who is Yahweh Himself, *best* demonstrated God's presence by living among us. *He is* the one who is always with us (Matthew 28:20).

1. How are we often like Moses in our response to God's call to serve?

2. As you look back upon your life, how has God prepared, sustained, and encouraged you as you have faced difficult situations?

3. Examine the " I AM" statements in John's Gospel. Which are especially meaningful to you? How is "I AM" and His power evident in your life today—in your words, your thoughts, your actions?

4. How is "I AM" and His power evident in your congregation today? How might God use members of your group to accomplish His purposes for your congregation?

5. If we're honest, we must confess that we often resist, ignore, or deny God's desire for us and our lives. For these and all other sins Jesus went to the cross to suffer and die. God's love for us, revealed in the person and work of Jesus, empowers and motivates us to respond to "I AM" with the statement, "I will." As you look to the future, how will the power of "I AM" be revealed in what you say and what you do?

Catechism Connection

Examine the First Article of the Apostles' Creed and Martin Luther's explanation in the opening for this session.

1. Luther's explanation teems with gifts from our Creator. Which gifts seem especially precious when a child is born? when we're seeking a job? when one of our children is sick? during a storm?

2. In the Large Catechism Martin Luther says that "if we believed [the First Article] with our whole heart, we would also act accordingly, and not swagger about and brag and boast as if we had life, riches, power, honor, and such things of ourselves, as if we ourselves were to be feared and served" (LC II:21). How can we grow in our power to believe the Article "with our whole heart"?

3. How will this faith affect our response when God says, "I choose you to carry out this task"?

Send

To Do This Week

Family Connection

1. Share with your children how God has empowered and sustained you even as you have faced difficult situations. Work together to make a "Thank You God" poster.

2. Discuss the story of the call of Moses. Compare your responses to serve God with Moses' responses. Then speak the words, "God promises, 'I am with you.'"

3. Consider a new way that you as a family might serve God together. Spell out the details of the plan.

Personal Reflection

1. Review the "I AM" passages from John's Gospel: John 6:35; 8:58; 9:5; 10:7; 10:11; 11:25; 14:6; and 15:1. Consider all that God reveals about Himself to you through the person, work, and words of Jesus.

2. As you wake each morning and retire each night, pray that God would use you to serve Him.

3. Thank God that He is with you always.

For Next Week

Read Exodus 5:1–12:30 in preparation for the next session.

Session 2

God Works to Deliver His People from Egypt

(Exodus 5:1–12:30)

Gather

Theme: Flexing His Muscle

Key Point

God, whose mighty power rescued His people from Egypt and also rescued us from the power of Satan, also enables us to confess in faith, "Jesus Christ is Lord."

Objectives

By the power of the Holy Spirit working through God's Word, we will

1. describe how God "flexed His muscle" in order to deliver His people from Egypt;
2. confess our ignorance and defiance of God and His will;
3. praise God for the deliverance He provided us from sin, death, and the power of the devil through His Son's life, death, and resurrection.

Opening

Read responsively Psalm 33:12–22.

Leader: Blessed is the nation whose God is the LORD, the people He chose for His inheritance.

Participants: From heaven the LORD looks down and sees all mankind;

Leader: from His dwelling place He watches all who live on earth—

Participants: He who forms the hearts of all, who considers everything they do.

Leader: No king is saved by the size of his army; no warrior escapes by his great strength.

Participants: A horse is a vain hope for deliverance; despite all its great strength it cannot save.

Leader: But the eyes of the LORD are on those who fear Him, on those whose hope is in His unfailing love,

Participants: to deliver them from death and keep them alive in famine.

Leader: We wait in hope for the LORD; He is our help and our shield.

Participants: In Him our hearts rejoice, for we trust in His holy name. May Your unfailing love rest upon us, O LORD, even as we put our hope in You.

Introduction

The phrase *flexing his muscle* may describe a physiological event or the way a person acts when confronted with a difficult situation.

1. When might it be necessary or advantageous to "flex" your muscle?

2. Describe a time when you "flexed your muscle." What was the result?

In today's lesson we witness God "flexing His muscles" in order to deliver His people from Egypt. As you read the events leading up to the Exodus, think about how God has flexed His muscle on your behalf in order to rescue you from sin and death.

Study

Reading the Text

God's plan for Moses and the Israelites begins to unfold—but not without obstacles. In fact, Moses' first address to Pharaoh seems to make matters worse; Pharaoh adds to his slaves' load by forcing them to gather their own straw, a necessary binder for the clay bricks used in Pharaoh's building projects. Far from being a hero, Moses is rebuked by his own people (Exodus 5:1–21).

Nevertheless, God's salvation is being accomplished. Pharaoh's sterner measures were probably necessary motivation for the Israelites to leave Egypt when the opportunity finally came (since even afterward they often wished to return; see 14:11–12; 16:3; 17:3; Numbers 14:2–4; 20:2–5). And God immediately speaks to Moses, reassuring him of His covenant with the people (Exodus 6:2–8). As He is the God of Abraham, Isaac, and Jacob, so with these children of Israel—He will be their God and they will be His chosen people. God reveals that His relationship with them will be more personal than it was with the patriarchs, for He has invited this young nation to call Him by His personal name, Yahweh, I AM (English translation, the LORD). Surely He will redeem them from bondage by flexing His muscles! (6:6).

The redemption takes place by means of ten plagues: (1) the Nile turned to blood (7:14–25); (2) frogs covering the land (8:1–15); (3) gnats (or, possibly, lice or mosquitoes, 8:16–19); (4) flies (most likely a large, biting variety, 8:20–32); (5) death of the livestock (perhaps by a disease like anthrax, 9:1–7); (6) boils (large, infectious sores, 9:8–12); (7) hail (9:13–35); (8) locusts (a dreaded pestilence in that region even today, 10:1–20); (9) darkness (10:21–29); and (10) the death of the firstborn (11:1–10, 12:29–30).

Naturalistic explanations are often offered for the plagues (e.g., an extraordinary Nile flood and its aftermath). The text certainly allows such possibilities. However, the text is emphatic that God was actively bringing about each plague at the moment of His decree (7:15–17; 8:9–10). Each plague was a miracle of God.

It is also significant that many of the plagues were directed toward the mythical gods honored by the Egyptians. For example, the Egyptians worshiped the Nile River (whom they believed was a god named Hopi), a frog (as the goddess, Heqt), and a bull-god (Apis). Thus when the Nile water became blood, when frogs overran the land and then died suddenly, and when the livestock perished, it demonstrated Yahweh's power over these false gods. Climactically, the ninth plague, darkness, warned the Egyptians that their chief deity, the sun god, Amon-Ra, was helpless to save them from the God of Israel.

The power of the plagues was overwhelming. At first, Pharaoh's magicians were able—no doubt by Satan's doing—to mimic God's signs (7:11–12; 7:22; 8:7). Yahweh, however, always maintained the upper hand (7:12). By the third plague God ceased to permit the imitations, finally putting the magicians to public humiliation (9:11). Moreover, the Lord left no doubt that it was Israel's God at work, conspicuously sparing His people from the suffering (8:22–23; 9:4–7; 9:26; 10:23; 11:7). Eventually Pharaoh's own advisors and all the Egyptians were willing to submit to Yahweh, Moses, and the Israelites (8:19; 10:7; 11:2–3).

Why, then, would Pharaoh not yield? If, as is likely, these events took place in 1447–1446 B.C., the Pharaoh would have been Amenhotep II. This young king, who had ascended the throne three years earlier at age 18, was the badly-spoiled son of Hatshepsut's step-son, Thutmose III. Obviously, he was a stubborn young man.

Yet there is more to Pharaoh's resistance. God hardened his heart (9:12; 10:1, 20, 27; 11:10). Why? To display His power as a warning for the good of the Egyptians as well as for the encouragement and liberation of Israel (7:3–5). God did not want to sacrifice Pharaoh; God did not desire his destruction. Indeed, God desires to save all people (1 Timothy 2:4)! In reality, God made His demands upon Pharaoh as reasonable as possible; Moses' initial request was only that Pharaoh grant the people temporary leave to worship (Exodus 5:1–3).

Unfortunately for him, Pharaoh refused God's demands. Pharaoh's heart was hardened *before* God acted against him (7:13, 22; 8:19; 9:7). Before God actively hardened Pharaoh's heart, Pharaoh repeatedly hardened his own (8:15, 32; 9:34). This is the danger of resisting God. While the Lord earnestly gives forgiveness and life to everyone in His Word and Sacraments, those who steadfastly refuse the gift He may finally harden. (Those who fear that God has hardened their hearts can be sure that God has not, because that very fear is certain evidence of God working in the heart. A truly hardened heart is always totally unconcerned about God's Word and will.)

Pharaoh's resistance could only be crushed by the ultimate plague, the death of the firstborn son in every house of Egypt (11:1–6). Remarkably, such a terrible judgment gave occasion for the most dramatic act of deliverance in the Old Testament (12:1–30). While the angel of death brought devastating punishment upon sin, his passing over the homes of the faithful vividly expressed God's solution for sin and death. The Old Testament offers no clearer picture of the salvation God gives in Christ Jesus than in the "Passover."

The image of Christ in the Passover is vivid. Every Israelite family was to observe the historic night with a special meal of a spotless male lamb (12:5). Jesus, the Lamb of God (John 1:29), was spotless, without sin. The blood of the Passover lamb was to be spread on the doorposts and over the lintel (Exodus 12:7); the vertical posts and horizontal lintel can remind us of the shape of a cross. Only bread without yeast was to be eaten at the meal (12:8); cleansing the house of leaven symbolizes the washing away of sin, just as Jesus cleanses us from all sin (1 John 1:7). Above all, when the angel of death saw the lamb's blood on the door, he would pass over, sparing the house (Exodus 12:13); the blood of Christ saves us from eternal death (1 Peter 1:18–21).

For generations to come, this Passover meal would remind believers of Israel that someday their Savior would come as the final Passover lamb. In the meantime, it marked the mighty act that would at long last free them from slavery.

Discussing the Text

1. How did God flex His muscle in each plague? What do His actions reveal about Himself?

2. How did the plagues challenge Pharaoh's belief in the power of his gods?

3. Compare and contrast the actions of the Israelites in Exodus 5:19–21 and 12:27b–28. How do you account for this change?

4. How does Passover foreshadow the person and work of Jesus?

Apply

Ultimately, God will bring His purpose to completion for all people, whether for destruction (their stubborn choice) or for salvation (God's gracious gift). In the beginning, Pharaoh proudly asserted, "I do not know the LORD and I will not let Israel go" (Exodus 5:2). By the end of the lesson, he knew the Lord's power only too well and begged the Israelites to leave (12:31). The price of Pharaoh's resistance, though, was the devastation of his kingdom.

Many people live in ignorance of God. Others openly defy His power. But the day will come when every knee will bow and every tongue will confess that Jesus Christ is the almighty Lord of the universe (Philippians 2:10–11). No one can resist God forever. Everyone will be brought into submission in the end. For those who have remained in opposition, this will mean eternal suffering in hell.

Such a destination, however, is not God's desire for anyone. God wishes to use His almighty power only for the good—the eternal salvation—of every soul. The overwhelming power of the plagues brought Israel out of Egypt. God's power to kill also revealed His mercy to save, as He protected the Israelites from the angel of death. This same mercy He has extended to everyone through His own Passover Lamb, Jesus Christ. As we trust in the Lord, His mighty power will be at work to save us from every day's dangers, frustrations, and difficulties—and especially from our sins.

In studying this lesson, we become aware that we may not trifle with God, for He is the Lord of our lives. But above all, we know that the Lord of the universe wields awesome power for us!

1. What is the spiritual outcome for those who live in ignorance of God? for those who openly defy Him?

2. What did the children of Israel do to deserve the deliverance God provided them? What have we done to deserve the deliverance God has provided us?

3. Compare and contrast the Lord's Supper with the Passover meal.

4. In Colossians 2:16–17 St. Paul says that the Passover and other Old Testament festivals were a shadow of the things that were to come. In what ways is a *shadow* fitting imagery?

5. How can and do you praise God for flexing His muscle on your behalf to deliver you from sin and death?

6. How does the Lord continue to flex His muscle in your life today?

Catechism Connection

Review the First Article of the Apostles' Creed and Martin Luther's explanation in the opening for Session 1.

1. During recent years Christians have experienced terrorist attacks, war, hurricanes, earthquakes, forest fires, and other tragedies. Yet, Luther assures us that God "defends me against all danger and guards and protects me from all evil." How can we believe Luther's words? See also Romans 8:18–39.

2. In Psalm 73 the author (Asaph) tells about questions he had regarding God's care of the righteous. How did his perspective change when he "entered the sanctuary of God" (verse 17)? What assurances for us do you find in verses 18–28?

Send

To Do This Week

Family Connection

1. For children, the fact that God sent plagues may cause some discomfort. Ask, "How could a loving God send plagues?" After discussing the issue, remind your children that God desired to deliver His people from persecution and in so doing desires to proclaim Himself as God. The people of Egypt had many opportunities to turn from their false gods and follow the one true God as they witnessed His power.

2. Discuss the blessings and power God provides us today in His holy meal, the Lord's Supper. In the Lord's Supper, Jesus gives us His body and His blood, in, with, and under bread and wine, to provide us forgiveness of sins and eternal life.

3. Create a family psalm to praise God for the deliverance He has provided through the person and work of His only Son Jesus.

4. Read Romans 8:31b–32 during your family devotions each day this week.

Personal Reflection

1. Consider this week the magnitude of God's love for you—He sent His only Son into this world to suffer and die for your sins.

2. Take time this week to share with someone how God flexed His muscle on your behalf.

For Next Week

Read Exodus 12:31–42 and 13:17–15:21 in preparation for the next session.

Session 3

God Leads His People Out of Egypt

(Exodus 12:31–42; 13:17–15:21)

Gather

Theme: Follow the Leader

Key Point

God desires that we follow Him wherever He may lead.

Objectives

By the power of the Holy Spirit working through God's Word, we will

1. describe how God led His people out of Egypt;
2. confess that we often fail to follow God;
3. thank God for His perfectly executed plan to rescue us from the clutches of sin and death through the person and work of Jesus.

Opening

Read the Second Commandment and Martin Luther's explanation responsively:

Group: You shall not misuse the name of the Lord your God.
Leader: What does this mean?
Group: We should fear and love God so that we do not curse, swear, use satanic arts, lie, or deceive by His name, but call upon it in every trouble, pray, praise, and give thanks.

Introduction

Children enjoy playing follow the leader. Players choose one person to be the leader. Then whatever the leader does or says all participants must say or do.

Adults also play follow the leader. Unfortunately, at times the leader whom adults follow may lead them away from God and His will for their lives.

1. Consider the consequences of following these leaders.

a. alcohol and drugs

b. sex

c. money

d. material possessions

e. job

2. What other leaders might people follow? What are some consequences of following these leaders?

3. God says, "You shall have no other gods before Me" (Exodus 20:3). If you follow anything or anyone other than the one true God, you break the First Commandment. Why do you suppose people, including yourself, have so much difficulty following the one true Leader?

In the lesson for today, the Israelite people follow God, the one true Leader, out of Egypt. In His perfectly executed plan, God delivers His people out of the clutches of Pharaoh. In His perfectly executed plan, God delivers people today from the clutches of sin and death.

Study

Reading the Text

Just as the Passover was among the Old Testament's most vivid preenactments of the death of Christ, so the Exodus from Egypt was a dramatic prefiguring of Jesus' resurrection. The Exodus (from the Greek for "departure" or "exit") marks Israel's "Independence Day." It illustrates in a grand way the defeat of evil, escape from certain death, and emergence into new life.

After the deaths of their firstborn males, the Egyptians compel God's people to leave immediately—"For otherwise we will all die!" (Exodus 12:33). The Israelites do not go empty-handed, however. God has caused the Egyptians to give them gold, silver, and clothing (12:35–36). While this had the effect of "plundering the Egyptians," it may in some cases also have been an act of faith by the givers. Very likely some Egyptians believed that Yahweh would be merciful to them through His people Israel. No doubt God used these powerful events to save also some of the "enemy."

Moses, the author of Exodus, emphasizes God's design in all this when he writes that Israel left Egypt after 430 years "to the very day" (12:41; compare also Genesis 15:13 for a round number prophecy). This dates the Exodus at 1446 B.C. (if Joseph brought his father to Egypt in 1876). Joseph himself had trusted that the Lord would someday bring his family out of Egypt, for he had asked that they take his remains up with them (Exodus 13:19; Genesis 50:24–25).

It is difficult to imagine such a "mixed multitude" moving out together, likely more than 2 million people: 600,000 Israelite men plus women and children, additional foreigners who had attached themselves to the nation, and all their livestock (Exodus 12:37–38). Modern armies move in no more than hundreds of thousands. The Midianites of Gideon's day (some 200 years later) are described as "thick as locusts," more than "the sand of the seashore," though they numbered "only" 135,000 (Judges 7:12; 8:10). A movement of

2 million people and millions of animals compares to a metropolitan area the size of Toronto or Minneapolis-St. Paul suddenly abandoning home and factory and setting off into the country. To supply even the most basic of services—from water to food to sleeping quarters—was a mind-boggling achievement!

Yet set off they did—and not in chaos, but in a well-ordered march (Exodus 13:18). God directed every step, leading the Israelites visibly in a great, fiery pillar (13:21–22). By day, the people saw the cloud of smoke emanating from the Lord's blazing glory. By night, the fire itself lighted their way. As in other Old Testament appearances, the pillar was likely a revealing of God the Son. (The reference to the "angel," i.e., "messenger," of God in 14:19 recalls the "angel of the LORD," actually the Lord Himself, who had spoken to Moses from the burning bush, 3:2, 4.) Throughout the Old Testament, some of God's most dramatic appearances came in forms like this fiery, cloudy pillar (Exodus 16:10–12; 24:16–18; 40:34; Numbers 16:19–32; 1 Kings 8:10–11; Ezekiel 43:4–5).

By what route the Lord led His people has never been clearly established. They did not go the shortest way, due east along the Mediterranean shore, because God knew an immediate confrontation with enemies there would bring despair (Exodus 13:17). Instead they trekked south until, almost inexplicably, the Lord ordered them to turn back to the north (14:2). In fact, God had His reasons: Pharaoh, regretting his decision to release the Israelites, would see them apparently lost and wandering and decide to give chase. This would afford an opportunity for God to solidify His people in their faith (14:3–9).

The great confrontation took place somewhere near the Gulf of Suez, a northern finger of the Red Sea. The Hebrew text literally indicates the Sea of Reeds, not the main channel of the Red Sea (which is 200 miles across and averages 2,000 feet deep), but rather a shallower body above it.

Of course, the Creator of the universe could have divided an *ocean* if that had suited His purpose. What He did do was quite enough to accomplish His ends. The sea was wide enough for an entire army to enter at once (14:23). The water was high enough to be called "a wall" on either side as the Israelites passed through (14:22). And when the waters returned, they were deep enough to drown Pharaoh's forces. (Imagine the terror of the Egyptians when the Lord "looked down from the pillar of fire" upon them and threw them into confusion [14:24]. "It is a terrifying thing to fall into the hands of the living God.... For our God is a consuming fire" [Hebrews 10:31; 12:29].)

So mighty was God's miracle that news soon spread to the surrounding nations, just as Moses prophesied (Exodus 15:14–16). While most of these peoples resisted God by fighting His chosen ones, at least a few begged His mercy and were saved (Joshua 2:10–13; 9:8–9).

Just as important, God's miracle fortified the faith of His own people (Exodus 14:31). Such an awesome moment caused the Israelites to burst into song (15:1–21). At least for now, they were certain God would bring them into the Promised Land (15:17).

Discussing the Text

1. What miraculous events did God orchestrate in order to deliver His people from Egypt?

2. What did these events prove about God's leadership?

3. How would these events be important to the people during their journey to the Promised Land? How did God use these events hundreds of years later? See Nehemiah 9:10–12; Jeremiah 32:21; and Daniel 9:15.

4. How did the people respond to the deliverance God's leadership provided (see Exodus 15:1–21)?

31

Apply

The Exodus became for Israel the banner event of God's salvation. Over and over they would call to mind this demonstration of His might, used to save His people (Joshua 4:23; Nehemiah 9:11; Psalm 66:6; 78:13; Hebrews 11:29). The Christian church, too, has seen these events as illustrating God's deliverance—specifically foreshadowing the salvation brought by Christ's resurrection at Easter. The overthrow of Pharaoh's army is seen as a picture of Satan's defeat when Jesus rose from the dead. Israel's escape after being hopelessly hemmed in by the sea illustrates the resurrection's deliverance from certain death. God's people emerging through the Red Sea prefigures the new life we have because Jesus came back to life. So significant is the deliverance of Israel that believers will continue to sing of it in heaven (Revelation 15:3)!

Through faith in Jesus, we are assured of our own resurrection at the Last Day. As God did the impossible for Israel, He will do the impossible for us—raising us to life. As the Lord fought for Israel (Exodus 14:14), so we can keep silent and trust that He will defeat Satan for us. We will live forever—and that includes every day on earth, during which the mighty God will always protect and lead us.

1. How has God demonstrated His leadership in your life?

2. The people of Israel passed through the waters of the Red Sea. They were given a new life, free from the slavery they experienced in Egypt. Compare the waters of Holy Baptism to the waters which the people of Israel passed through.

3. How might you recount God's gracious deliverance like Moses and Miriam did in their song of praise, thanking God for the deliverance He has provided you from death?

4. Read Hebrews 11:24–29 and 11:39–12:2. What perspective does the writer to the Hebrews bring to the Exodus account?

Catechism Connection

Examine the Second Commandment and Martin Luther's explanation in the opening for this session.

1. Note the ways Moses and the Israelites honored God's name in Exodus 15:1–6. When and how can we honor God's name today?

2. What special uses of God's name do we find in Psalm 50:15; 103:1; and 118:1?

Send

To Do This Week

Family Connection

1. Review the events of the Exodus. Focus on God's activity in the lives of His people. You may wish to draw a family picture or create a family book to show the events of the Exodus.

2. Review the events of God's activity in the lives of each member of your family. Include such significant events as your Baptism, instruction in the faith, confirmation, and receiving the Lord's Supper. Tell your children what each of these events means to you.

3. Write a family song of praise for God's leadership and deliverance like the one by Moses and Miriam (Exodus 15:1–21).

4. God wants to be the leader in your family. Discuss specific ways that you can be sure that God remains the leader. Consider Bible study, devotions, Bible reading, prayer, and singing hymns.

Personal Reflection

1. Reread Exodus 15:1–21. Meditate on how the Lord has worked mightily in your life.

2. Write "Follow the Leader" on a business card and place it in your wallet. Remember each time you see the message that God desires to be number one in your life.

3. Thank God each morning and evening for the leadership and deliverance He has provided to you through His Son's death on the cross.

For Next Week

Read Exodus 16–17 in preparation for the next class session.

Session 4

God Gives His People Food and Water

(Exodus 16–17)

Gather

Theme: Like a Broken Record

Key Point

Inspite of our grumbling, God promises to provide all that we need to sustain our lives.

Objectives

By the power of the Holy Spirit working through God's Word, we will

1. describe God's provision for the physical welfare of His people in the wilderness and His people's dissatisfaction, evident in their constant grumbling;
2. confess that we often grumble about that which God provides;
3. praise and thank God that He provides for all of our needs, including our greatest need—forgiveness of sins and eternal life—through His Son Jesus.

Opening

Read aloud, in unison, Isaiah 58:9–11.

> Then you will call and the LORD will answer;
> > you will cry for help, and He will say: Here am I.
> "If you do away with the yoke of oppression,
> > with the pointing finger and malicious talk,
> and if you spend yourselves in behalf of the hungry
> > and satisfy the needs of the oppressed,
> then your light will rise in the darkness,
> > and your night will become like the noonday.

> The LORD will guide you always;
>> He will satisfy your needs in a sun-scorched land
>> and will strengthen your frame.
> You will be like a well-watered garden,
>> like a spring whose waters never fail."

Introduction

"You sound like a broken record."

With CDs and cassette tapes it is difficult for some today to relate to this saying. But not so many years ago records played the music of the day. When a record became scratched or warped, the needle would stick and play the same few words and music over and over and over. Nothing seemed more annoying than a "broken record." Today when people use the phrase *You sound like a broken record,* they describe a person who does or says something over and over and over again.

1. Describe a time when you or someone you know sounded or acted like a broken record.

2. Compare sin to a broken record. For help read James 1:13–15.

God mightily and miraculously delivered the Israelites from Egypt. Not long after their deliverance the Israelites grumbled and complained like a broken record. In spite of their sinful rebellion, God in His love continued to provide for the needs of His people. God has repeated the message of His love more often than we have grumbled.

Study

Reading the Text

The Sinai Peninsula, the region in which Israel spent her wilderness years, is a triangular wedge of land approximately 230 miles long, north to south, and 110 miles across in the north, where it touches the Mediterranean Sea. To the south, it tapers to a point where the Gulf of Suez and the Gulf of Aqaba each join the Red Sea proper. Thus it is a relatively small territory (about the combined size of Vermont and New Hampshire) in which the Israelites moved for 40 years.

The land itself is perhaps not quite as we might envision it. One central belt of the peninsula is shifting sand (as in the Sahara), but to the north and south there is more vegetation. The southern portion in particular is very mountainous, including the peak we know as Mount Horeb, or Sinai. Few rivers flow year-round. Instead, many *wadis* rush as torrents after the occasional rains, and then quickly run dry. Water—a precious resource—is available in clusters of springs. Today, the peninsula supports a nomadic, Bedouin population of some size, but their existence is sparse. It is not by any means a hospitable land, particularly for a mass of 2 million people, grouped closely together, all in need of food and water.

Understandably, then, the land through which the Israelites were now passing seemed a bad exchange for the well-watered Nile delta they had just left. Less understandably, the people forgot the power God had shown so recently and began to grumble against Moses and Aaron (Exodus 16:1–3). This was, of course, actually rebellion against God (16:7–8). It would continue like a broken record throughout Israel's travels (14:11–12; 15:24; 17:2; Numbers 11:1; 14:2; 16:3; 21:5).

God is, however, incredibly patient! He answers Israel's ungratefulness with further generosity. Lest there be any mistake about the source, He has Moses announce that meat and bread will be provided shortly (Exodus 16:4–12).

In this part of the world, in the spring of the year, large flocks of quail sometimes fly northward to escape coming summer heat. This flyover, though, was extraordinary, both because the birds were so numerous and because they arrived precisely on cue

37

(16:12–13). They were easily captured and offered a welcome and bountiful buffet of protein. (For a second miracle of quail, see Numbers 11:31.)

The bread came in the morning (Exodus 16:13–21). Finding fine flakelike deposits on the ground, the Israelites asked in Hebrew, *"Man hu?"* or "What is it?"(16:15). Thus named *manna,* it could be boiled or baked to produce cakes tasting of honey and olive oil (16:31; Numbers 11:7–8). In many respects, it was like a naturally occurring substance produced by the tamarisk trees of this region. When pricked by a tiny insect, the trees drop a honey-like globule, which is edible but quickly melts in the hot sun.

In other ways, the manna from heaven was like nothing the Israelites had ever seen. It occurred year-round, wherever the people traveled, for the next 40 years, until the Israelites reached the Promised Land. (The natural substance from the tamarisk trees develops only from about May through July.) The manna was sufficient in quantity to feed millions, while the tamarisks of the entire peninsula produce only about 700 pounds a year. Most strikingly, the miraculous manna appeared *six* days a week and skipped every seventh day (the Sabbath).

In this way, God was able to "test," or teach, His people to trust Him (16:4). From Sunday through Thursday, only as much as could be eaten in one day would remain fresh (16:19–21); the people were forced to rely on God to provide anew the next morning. On the other hand, by God's command, no work was to be done on the Sabbath. The Israelites then gathered twice the usual amount on Friday, and by God's hand that food remained edible the following day (16:22–30). One day's ration, an "omer" or a "tenth of an ephah" (16:36), is variously calculated as from one to two quarts.

The other necessity for survival was water. Once before the people had been thirsty, and God had intervened (15:22–25). Now Moses was told to strike "the rock at Horeb" to bring forth water (17:5–6). (The definite reference to *the* rock suggests a very large, bare outcropping of rock, like the summit of a hill, rather than a single boulder as often depicted.) In the presence of several witnesses—elders of Israel—God again proved His greatness and goodness, and He validated Moses' leadership.

Discussing the Text

1. Read Exodus 16:11–15. How did God miraculously provide for the basic needs of His people?

2. How did God's provision indicate to His people their value to Him? How did the people respond to that which the Lord provided (Numbers 11:4–6)?

3. What did the Lord teach His people by providing manna six days a week and then skipping the seventh day (the Sabbath)?

4. According to Deuteronomy 8:1–4, what purpose did God have for allowing the people to get hungry and then feeding them with manna? How do we know that God did not intend this to be only a one-time lesson? See, for example, 1 Kings 8:56–59 and Nehemiah 9:20–21.

Apply

Looking back on these incidents, Moses later reminded the Israelites, "The Lord humbled you, causing you to hunger and then feeding you with manna, … to teach you that man does not live on bread alone, but on every word that comes from the mouth of the Lord" (Deuteronomy 8:3). Much later, recalling the same miracles, Jesus fed 5,000 and then called Himself "the bread of life ... that [came] down from heaven" (John 6:35–40).

Two clear applications may therefore be drawn. (1) We remember that daily bread is always a gift of God. In the Lord's Prayer we ask for daily bread (that is, all our earthly needs) so that we will recognize it as His gift and give Him thanks. We truly live by every word of the Lord, because material blessings come always and only when He says the word.

(2) When the Lord speaks earthly blessings, He is actually saying much more. God's feeding Israel kept alive His eternal covenant with them. Jesus fed the multitude, not just to sustain them to the morrow, but to enable them to believe in Him as the One who gives and sustains everlasting life. Every meal, every new dress, every CD or video is a reminder that Jesus gives Himself so that we may live with Him in heaven.

1. How do we, for whom the Lord has richly provided, sometimes act like the Israelites?

2. In Galatians 6:2 Paul admonishes us to carry one another's burdens. How can a member of a Christian congregation do this for fellow members who feel they have reasons to grumble?

3. How is God's love like a broken record?

4. For what greatest need has God provided for you? What is the significance of this provision?

5. How can you demonstrate your thankfulness to God for all He has provided? How do you demonstrate your thankfulness?

Catechism Connection

Review the Second Commandment and Martin Luther's explanation in the opening for Session 3.

1. What common evils are forbidden in James 3:9–10 and Leviticus 19:12?

2. Why do you think people resort to these sins so easily and often?

3. Summarize the guidelines Jesus provides for cursing and swearing in Matthew 5:33–37.

Send

To Do This Week

Family Connection

1. Review with your family the ways in which God provided for the people of Israel. Discuss how the Lord provides for your family.

2. Discuss the effects of grumbling and complaining on the members of your family, on the attitudes of people in your family, and its effect on accomplishing that which you desire.

3. Begin to create a list of the many blessings that God has provided for you. Include on your list the forgiveness and eternal life that Jesus won for you on the cross. Continue to add to the list on a daily basis. At mealtime, give thanks to God for each of the items on the list. Place your list in a conspicuous place in the house.

4. Pray together the Lord's Prayer. Discuss the sentence "Give us this day our daily bread."

Personal Reflection

1. Give thanks in the morning and evening for the blessings that God has provided for you.

2. Share with a friend or loved one all that the Lord has provided to you.

3. Meditate on the magnitude of God's love for you. He provides for all of your needs, including your greatest need—forgiveness of sins and eternal life.

For Next Week

Read Exodus 19:1–20:21; 24; 32; and 35:4–29 in preparation for the next session.

Session 5

God Helps Us Follow Him

(Exodus 19:1–20:21; 24; 32; 35:4–29)

— Gather —

Theme: Spelled Out

Key Point

God's love revealed in and through the person and work of Jesus on our behalf motivates us to desire to obey His commands.

Objectives

By the power of the Holy Spirit working through God's Word, we will

1. summarize the Ten Commandments God provided to the Israelites and to us in order to help us to follow Him;
2. confess that because of our sinful nature we are incapable of fulfilling perfectly God's expectations revealed in His Commandments;
3. desire to follow God as we are motivated by His love for us in Christ Jesus.

Opening

Read responsively the following selected verses from Psalm 51.

Leader: Have mercy on me, O God, according to Your unfailing love;

Participants: according to Your great compassion blot out my transgressions.

Leader: Wash away all my iniquity

Participants: and cleanse me from my sin.

Leader: For I know my transgressions,

Participants: and my sin is always before me.

Leader: Against You, You only, have I sinned

Participants: and done what is evil in Your sight,
Leader: so that You are proved right when You speak
Participants: and justified when You judge.
Leader: Surely I was sinful at birth,
Participants: sinful from the time my mother conceived me.
All: Create in me a pure heart, O God, and renew a steadfast spirit within me. Do not cast me from Your presence or take Your Holy Spirit from me. Restore to me the joy of Your salvation and grant me a willing spirit, to sustain me.

Introduction

1. Have you ever "spelled out" clearly your expectations only to have someone disregard or defy them? Describe the situation.

2. God "spelled out" clearly His expectations for us in the Ten Commandments. How do we disregard or defy them? Why is this (see Psalm 51:5)?

In today's lesson God spells out clearly His expectations for His people. Before long the people of Israel—the people God had rescued from Egypt, the people God had provided for, the people whom God loved and called to be His own—sin against God. Moses continually intercedes on behalf of the Israelites. Because of our sin, God has provided for us an intercessor—Jesus Christ—who came to earth to accomplish for us what we could never accomplish on our own—a restored relationship with God through His sacrificial death on the cross. We in turn desire to do that which God has spelled out in His Law.

Study

Reading the Text

Israel was free! Big sky above. Wide-open space ahead. Freedom did not mean, however, that God intended for Israel to *go* anywhere, to *do* anything, to *be* anything. God had freed this nation to be His nation—and to be the nation through which He would carry out His plans for the whole world. Therefore, in today's lesson, God establishes with the children of Israel a unique covenant, setting them apart to be His own people.

From the outset of their journey, God has been leading Israel to a specific destination (Exodus 3:12). Very quickly, in just the third month out of Egypt (19:1–2), they reach it: Mount Sinai, the place where God had first called Moses from the burning bush. The probable site of the biblical mountain is a peak in the southeastern portion of the Sinai Peninsula. From a large plain already 5,000 feet above sea level, it rises abruptly another 2,000. The location provided an ideal campsite for the huge throng, as well as a stunning "pulpit" from which God could speak. Israel would remain there for 11 months.

Immediately God states His purpose for bringing the people to this point, for everything He has done for them. He has carried them "as on eagles' wings" so that they can be for Him "a kingdom of priests and a holy nation" (19:4–6). For the next 1,400 years, this is Israel's mission statement. Being priests means being the go-between from God to the rest of the world. Through Israel, God works His plan of sending everyone's Savior, the Messiah.

The terms under which Israel is to live out her calling are spelled out in the Ten Commandments (20:1–17). The commandments express a covenant, as was common among the ancients, in which a greater king takes lesser kings to be his own. God establishes the covenant by what He has already done for Israel (20:2). Israel merely receives His kindness and agrees to live on His terms.

Clearly, when God gives His commandments, He means business! The Israelites were to prepare for three days (19:10–15). Then, when God spoke, the thunder, the lightning, the earthquake, and the trumpet so terrified the people that they begged

Moses to intercede for them (19:16–19; 20:18–19). This was exactly as God wished (Deuteronomy 5:28). He meant His appearance to be a powerful deterrent to sin (the "first use of the Law"; Exodus 20:20). More important, He wished to impress upon the people their need for an intercessor, or mediator, someone to restore their relationship with God. The Law was to serve as a mirror (the "second use of the Law") to show people their sin. Compared to the divine holiness, every person falls short of God's glory and stands in dread of His righteous demands.

Once stricken with an awareness of sin and their separation from God, souls are eager for someone to step in. In these texts, Moses illustrates that role. Time and time and time again he ascends the mountain, speaks to God on behalf of the people, and then returns (19:3ff.; 20:21; 24:3, 12; 32:15, 30).

This *vicarious atonement*—a relationship restored through a mediator—is especially visualized when Moses comes down the mountain to present the book of the covenant, an elaboration of the Ten Commandments, spoken by God (20:22–23:33). The people promise, "All that the Lord has spoken, we will do" (24:3). The Law would serve as a guide, or rule (the "third use of the Law"), for following God's commands. Sacrifices are offered. Then Moses sprinkles the blood on the *altar and on the people,* thereby reconnecting the two (24:5–8). Now, remarkably, the elders are able to enter God's presence without fear and without punishment (24:9–11).

The analogy to Jesus Christ is unmistakable. By coming to earth, the Son of God became the Mediator between God and humankind (1 Timothy 2:5). By His death, Christ took the punishment which we must bear if we stand before God on our own—in our sinfulness. And by the shedding of His blood, the blood of the new covenant (Matthew 26:28), Jesus enables us to come into God's presence without fear of judgment (Hebrews 10:19–22).

Moses' most dramatic act of intercession comes 40 days later. Having trusted in "this fellow Moses" rather than in the Lord, the people panic when their leader remains so long on the mountain (Exodus 32:1). They sin in demanding a visible representation of God—something He had specifically forbidden (Exodus 20:4)—

rather than being content with the ways God had chosen to reveal Himself. Although the golden calf is meant to be Yahweh (32:5), it is a grievous sin against the First Commandment, because it reduces God to being only what man imagines Him to be. With the corrupted worship also comes drunken, sexual orgy (32:6).

So quickly Israel has shattered God's covenant! The smashing of the stone tablets symbolizes this broken covenant (32:19). God is ready to destroy the entire nation and start over with Moses (32:7–10), but twice more Moses steps in (32:11–13, 30–32). Moses pleads on the basis of protecting God's own honor (32:12) and on the basis of His promises to the fathers (32:13). Moses is even willing to take the place of the people in eternal damnation (32:32).

Marvelously, God changes His mind (32:14). How can that be? God, of course, knows everything in advance—what He will do and why. Yet He does what He does through the prayers of His people. The prayers of God's children make a difference. To paraphrase one Christian pastor, "For the believers' sake God gives to, and preserves for, the world all it has."

Such great forgiveness motivates great love (see Luke 7:47). The children of Israel later demonstrate their grateful love in donations for the building of the tabernacle (Exodus 35:4–29). No one was coerced to give; all offerings were to come from a "willing heart" (35:5). Yet the people gave so much that Moses actually had to restrain them from giving more (36:4–6)! So powerful is God's Good News!

Discussing the Text

1. List the Ten Commandments (Exodus 20:3, 7, 8, 12, 13, 14, 15, 16, 17a, 17b). What do they tell us to *do* and *not to do*?

2. What are the three uses of the Law? How is each important?

First use:

Second use:

Third use:

3. Why was it necessary for Moses to intercede on behalf of the people of Israel? How is Jesus our intercessor? Why is it necessary for Jesus to intercede for us?

4. Examine Hebrews 10, especially verses 1, 11–14, and 19–22. What additional insights do you find about the relationship of Moses and Jesus?

Apply

In calling, saving, and guiding Israel, God was taking for Himself people to carry out His saving plan on earth. Since the coming of Christ, we, the Christian church, are God's "chosen people, a royal priesthood, a holy nation" (1 Peter 2:9). In a new way, we are to "declare the praises of Him who called [us] out of darkness into His wonderful light."

Like the Israelites, we have done nothing to establish God's new covenant with us. In fact, on our own we are dead in transgressions and sins (Ephesians 2:1). But Christ is the Mediator, who by His blood restored our relationship with God. The Holy Spirit has called us to be God's people, a holy nation, by Baptism. This gives us immense reason to be thankful, to respond to Him with acts of love and obedience—all those acts the Ten Commandments prescribe. We are free, but not free to do whatever we wish. Rather, in living according to God's commands, we are His new go-betweens to the world. We have the privilege and honor of being God's priests—showing, telling, and reminding others of the Savior.

1. Describe the covenant God has established with us. Summarize what this means for you.

2. Read 2 Corinthians 5:14–15. Why do Christians desire to do that which God commands?

3. How are we "free, but not free"? See Romans 6:20–22 and Galatians 5:13–14.

Catechism Connection

Review the First Article of the Apostles' Creed and Martin Luther's explanation in the opening for Session 1.

1. Read Exodus 36:2–7. How did the people "thank and praise, serve and obey" God?

2. Read Psalm 116:12–14, 17–18. How did the psalmist choose to repay the Lord for all His goodness to him?

3. What type of response to God's goodness does Paul encourage in 2 Corinthians 9:10–11?

Send

To Do This Week

Family Connection

1. Discuss each of the Ten Commandments. Ask, "What does God want us to do? What does God not want us to do?" Work together to make a poster of one of the commandments.

2. Tell your children of God's expectation for them described in Matthew 5:48, "Be perfect." Ask, "How well are you living up to the expectations that God has spelled out for you?" Remind your children that God knew they would be unable to do that which He expected. That's why God sent Jesus into this world—to meet perfectly the expectations that God had for us, and then to suffer the punishment we deserved because of our sin.

3. Ask, "How did the people of Israel break the First Commandment? How do we break the First Commandment?"

Personal Reflection

1. Meditate on Psalm 51.

2. Consider ways in which you can respond in thankfulness and praise to God for the forgiveness He won for you through His Son's death on the cross.

3. Share God's expectations with a friend or loved one. Then take time to tell how God fulfilled that which we could never accomplish on our own—forgiveness of sins and eternal life through faith in Christ Jesus.

For Next Week

Read Numbers 21:4–9 and Joshua 3–4 in preparation for the next session.

Session 6

God Saves His People

(Numbers 21:4–9; Joshua 3–4)

Gather

Theme: Lifted Up—Uplifted

Key Point

God, who saved the Israelites from death, sent His only Son to save us from eternal death.

Objectives

By the power of the Holy Spirit working through God's Word, we will

1. describe how God saved His people from death;
2. compare God's deliverance of His people in the wilderness to the deliverance He provides through the person and work of Jesus;
3. seek opportunities to receive the faith-strengthening power of the Holy Spirit offered freely in God's Word and Sacrament.

Opening

Read the First Commandment and Martin Luther's explanation.

All: You shall have no other gods.

Leader: What does this mean?

All: We should fear, love, and trust in God above all things.

Introduction

"He gave me a *lift*."
"He *lifted* my spirits."
"I was *uplifted* by His Word."
"He was *lifted up* on a cross."

1. Describe the meaning of the first three statements using a situation you or someone you know experienced.

2. How does the last statement suggest the means to the end described in the first three statements?

In today's lesson we once again observe the gross sins of the Israelites against the One who had delivered them, sustained them, and loved them. They stumbled and fell. We also witness the long patience and mercy of God, who continues to forgive His people for their sin and leads them to the land He has promised them. God lifted up His people. Why? All this God provides purely out of His grace—undeserved love.

Study

Reading the Text

So much has happened! The children of Israel remained camped before Mount Sinai for 11 months. While there, they dedicated the tabernacle (Exodus 40), ordained their first priests (Leviticus 8), and began the worship customs that would continue throughout the Old Testament.

From Sinai, they had reached the border of Canaan in short order, and spies had been sent into the land (Numbers 13–14). Tragically, 10 of the spies had discouraged the people with a frightening report. Rather than trust in the Lord and the good word of the other spies, Joshua and Caleb, the people rebelled. As a result, God decreed that this generation of Israelites would never enter the Promised Land; they would wander in the wilderness 40 years until all over the age of 20 died. Now, the wanderings are nearly over. Even Miriam and Aaron have died (Numbers 20). Israel again comes to Canaan.

One more disappointment awaits. Israel will enter the land from the east, by crossing the Jordan, but the nation of Edom blocks her way. God forbids Israel to attack the Edomites since they are relatives, descendants of Esau (Deuteronomy 2:1–7). Moses therefore leads the people south, once more *away* from Canaan, in order to circle around Edom. At this, they rebel again, murmuring against God and Moses (Numbers 21:4–5).

God responds by sending "fiery serpents" into the camp, and many die from their bites (21:6). These snakes were probably of a species still common in the Sinai today, identified by red wavy stripes and spots on their backs. They are *highly* poisonous. (The term *fiery* may refer to their markings or to the pain inflicted by their bites.)

God is, however, also quick to show mercy. As soon as the people repent, God instructs Moses to make a serpent of bronze (to resemble the color of the deadly snakes) and raise it up on a pole in the camp. Anyone who looks to the bronze serpent is healed of the snakebite (21:7–9).

The serpent on the pole illustrates Jesus being lifted up on the cross (John 3:14–15). All who look in faith to the cross of Jesus are healed from sin and eternal death. This kind of prophecy and fulfillment is called a "type" and "antitype." The Old Testament Scriptures specify a person, event, or institution—the type—to be a symbol of something in the New Testament—the antitype. (See Romans 5:14 and 1 Peter 3:21 for other examples.)

Having marched around Edom and Moab (another related people), the Israelites engage and defeat two Amorite kings on the east side of the Jordan (Numbers 21:10–35). This land later becomes the inheritance of two-and-a-half of the Israelite tribes. Israel then reaches the Jordan. One final time Moses addresses the people, reminding them of God's care these 40 years (the Book of Deuteronomy). Then, after gazing into the Promised Land from Mount Nebo, Moses dies (Deuteronomy 34).

Joshua takes command (Joshua 1:1–9). Now begins the big push. But between Israel and the prize is the swollen Jordan River (3:1). It is springtime, the days of Passover (4:19; 5:10) and of the early grain harvest (3:15), when snowmelt from Mount Hermon to the north always causes flooding. It is, therefore, also time for another miracle.

The priests are instructed to take the ark of the covenant ahead of the people and march toward the river (3:1–6). As God had specified (Exodus 25:10–15), the priests carry the ark, supported by two long poles, on their shoulders. The moment the priests set foot in the water, it subsides (Joshua 3:11–17). Thus, fittingly, the priests carrying the ark are first to reach the Promised Land, for the ark represents God's presence with His people. It is God Himself who will lead them into their new home.

Approximately 15 miles upriver (to the north), near the city of Adam (3:16), the flooded river has stood up, forming a wall. The water below that point, then, runs down as it always would into the Dead Sea, five miles further south. The whole nation, once again perhaps two million strong, crosses over on dry ground as the priests, holding the ark, stand patiently in the riverbed.

This miracle brings to mind the parting of the Red Sea 40 years earlier. But this time God is showing a new generation that He will also be with their new leader, Joshua (3:7). The message is not to be forgotten. Twelve stones from the riverbed are used to build a memorial on the opposite bank (4:1–9). (Some translations of 4:9 may also suggest that a second stone memorial was set up in the middle of the river.) In this way, future generations of Israelites, too, would learn of God's mighty deed (4:6–7, 20–24; see also Genesis 28:18; Joshua 22:10–34; 24:26–27; and 1 Samuel 7:12).

Discussing the Text

1. How did the spies' report (Number 13:28–33) discourage the people of Israel? How did the people of Israel respond (14:1–4)? How did God respond to the people's lack of trust(14:20–23)?

2. Read Numbers 21:4–9. Why did God send "fiery serpents" into the camp? How did God demonstrate His mercy to the people?

3. How did the serpent on the pole foreshadow the work of Jesus?

4. Why did God instruct the priests to take the ark of the covenant ahead of the people (Joshua 3:14)?

5. What did the parting of the river (3:15–17) demonstrate to the people of Israel?

Apply

The chief symbols in today's stories, the bronze serpent and the ark of the covenant, are powerful illustrations of the way God deals with us. In particular, the serpent on the pole was a means by which God gave blessings directly to people. In the very same way, God's Word, Baptism, and Holy Communion give us infinitely greater blessings—forgiveness and eternal life.

There was nothing magical about the bronze serpent. When the Israelites later thought so, it had to be destroyed (2 Kings 18:4). Likewise, words, water, and bread and wine do not work magically. But because God attaches His promises to them, all give what He declares. An Israelite could believe—without hesitation—that when he looked to the bronze serpent, God would restore his life. Just as surely, a person who hears and believes the promises of the Gospel has indeed been given life and forgiveness (John 20:23). A baby baptized or an adult receiving Communion has indeed been forgiven and granted heaven (Acts 2:38–39; Matthew 26:26–28). We may always believe this without doubt, because God has placed His blessings in these "means." When we believe the blessings, we have them!

We learn through today's texts the miraculous power of God to heal from deadly poison, to halt a flood, to forgive sins, and to give eternal life.

1. What means did God use to save the people of Israel (Numbers 21:8–9)?

2. As we look to the cross of Jesus Christ, what does God provide to us through faith?

3. God continues to use means to provide for the needs of His people. How does God use the following simple substances today: water, bread, and wine? What does God provide through each?

4. Compare Exodus 12:25–27 with Joshua 4:20–23. What concern is God addressing? What are some special times for us to tell our children about things God has done?

Catechism Connection

Examine the First Commandment and Martin Luther's explanation in the opening for this session.

1. Read Ephesians 5:5. What consequence awaits one who worships idols instead of God?

2. Note the types of idols mentioned in Philippians 3:19 and Revelation 9:20. What are some types of idolatry that are prevalent today?

3. What will surely happen if we attempt to fight idolatry with our own power? See Matthew 8:28 and 1 Peter 5:8.

Send

To Do This Week

Family Connection

1. Write "God Is Faithful" on three rocks, one word per rock. Talk about His faithfulness to Israel and to us.

2. Say, "God is present today." Ask, "How do we know that God is present today?" After a few responses remind your family that God is present today in, with, and under bread and wine in the Lord's Supper. God is present with us today in His Word.

3. Consider how your family might demonstrate the presence of God and His love to someone who may feel lonely, lost, or rejected. Devise a plan to share God's love with this person.

Personal Reflection

1. Plan to set aside time daily to be strengthened by the Word of God.

2. Meditate on how Jesus, who was lifted up on the cross, uplifts you from sin and from death.

3. Read all of Isaiah 63 as part of your personal devotions this week.

For Next Week

Review Joshua 3–4 and read 5:13–6:27 in preparation for the next session.

Session 7

God Gives Victory at Jericho

(Joshua 3–4; 5:13–6:27)

Gather

Theme: A Battle Won!

Key Point

Through Christ Jesus, God has emerged victorious over Satan, over our own sin, and over every other enemy we may encounter.

Objectives

By the power of the Holy Spirit working through God's Word, we will

1. describe the unconventional way God provided His people victory at Jericho;
2. recognize that forces exist today—our sinful self, the world, and Satan—that would tempt us to disobey God;
3. affirm that Jesus conquered sin, death, and the power of Satan when He died on the cross;
4. praise and thank Jesus, who continues to battle against the forces that would lead us astray.

Opening

Read responsively Psalm 129:1–4.

Leader: They have greatly oppressed me from my youth—let Israel say—

Participants: they have greatly oppressed me from my youth, but they have not gained the victory over me.

Leader: Plowmen have plowed my back and made their furrows long.

Participants: But the LORD is righteous; He has cut me free from the cords of the wicked.

Introduction
"Choose your battles wisely."

1. Describe a situation when you heard or spoke these words.

2. How can these words be good advice?

3. What battles are you unable to choose?

God knew that on their own the people of Israel would be unable to defeat the city of Jericho in battle. Guided by God, the Israelites defeated the Canaanites in Jericho. We, too, are unable on our own to win the battle against our enemies—our sinful self, the world and its temptations, and Satan. God, in His love for us, chose to do battle against all that would lead us away from Him. Through Jesus' death and resurrection God won the battle for us, giving us the assurance of forgiveness of sin and eternal life.

Study

Reading the Text

For commentary on Joshua 3–4, Israel crossing the Jordan, see Session 6.

After a brief rest and celebration of the Passover (Joshua 5:10), Joshua knows he must immediately advance against Jericho. But how? Jericho, the first city on Israel's path into Canaan, is also one of Canaan's strongest. Modern excavations suggest that the ancient city was surrounded by two walls, one six-feet, the other twelve-feet thick, each about thirty-feet high. Israel had no experience whatsoever in assaulting a walled fortress.

As he is considering—perhaps praying about—the nation's next move, Joshua is confronted by a mighty warrior whose sword is drawn (5:13–6:5). The stranger is neither an Israelite nor a Canaanite, but rather "the commander of the army of the LORD" (5:14). It is another appearance by the "angel of Yahweh," the Son of God, who identifies Himself as the Lord (6:2). Joshua is told to remove his sandals at this holy place (5:15), just as Moses had been instructed to do before the burning bush (Exodus 3:5). This is the very encouragement Joshua needs: The same God who was with Moses is now visibly with him!

God delivers the battle plan, a most unusual one (Joshua 6:2–5). There is to be neither a frontal attack, nor a siege of weapons, nor months of waiting to starve out the defenders. Seven priests with seven trumpets will lead the people, who will march around the city once each day for seven days. On that seventh day, they are to march around the city seven times, blow the trumpets, and shout. God will take care of the rest. One of these seven days, presumably the final one, would, of course, be a Sabbath. Though the Israelites were prohibited from working on the Sabbath, exception would always be made when doing what was truly God's business (compare Exodus 31:12–17 with Matthew 12:1–14).

Understanding that it would be God fighting the battle, Joshua follows orders precisely. If, as the ruins suggest, ancient Jericho was roughly 400-yards long by 200-yards wide, a march at a safe distance around the perimeter would be approximately a mile long. By the seventh day, the trip would be nearly seven miles. Israel marches on by faith, God's priests and the ark of the Lord always ahead of her (6:6; see also Hebrews 11:30).

Finally, at the moment of God's choosing, Joshua gives the command. The priests blow their trumpets, the warriors shout, and the walls fall down flat (6:15–21). The entire perimeter collapses; Israelite soldiers are able to charge from all angles (6:20). (For other instances in which trumpets announce the Lord's coming, see Exodus 19:16–20:18; Leviticus 23:23–27; 25:8–12; Isaiah 27:13; and, especially, Matthew 24:29–31; 1 Corinthians 15:51–52; 1 Thessalonians 4:15–17.)

God's decree is that everything in Jericho be devoted ("under the ban") to Him (6:17–19). Precious and useful metals are collected for the service of the tabernacle. Everything and everyone else is to be utterly destroyed. Men, women, and children are killed, lest they lead Israel into worshiping their gods (Deuteronomy 20:16–18). Animals, foodstuffs, and clothing are burned. In other conquered cities, God will allow His people to keep these spoils (Joshua 8:2). This city, the first conquest, is to be a firstfruits offering to the Lord (cf. Deuteronomy 26:1–11). In fact, the walls of Jericho are to lie in ruins as a permanent reminder of God's judgment. Joshua curses anyone who seeks to rebuild them (6:26), and six centuries later, in the wicked era of King Ahab, the curse will be carried out (1 Kings 16:33–34).

Only one family is spared. Rahab, a prostitute, had earlier harbored two Israelite spies (2:1–21). Now she and all those in her house are safely escorted out of the rubble. "By faith," Hebrews 11:31 says, "the prostitute Rahab, because she welcomed the spies, was not killed with those who were disobedient." Having heard of the mighty works of Israel's God, Rahab realized that only He could save her from perishing with the city. This faith she had then expressed by joining herself to God's people, even as her neighbors were fighting against them. And what a blessed result! After a period of ceremonial preparation outside the camp (Joshua 6:23), Rahab became fully incorporated into the chosen nation, marrying Salmon, a prince of Judah. Only much later would God's ultimate plan for Rahab be fulfilled: one of her descendants would be the Savior of all nations (Matthew 1:5–16).

Discussing the Text

1. Who developed the battle plan for the people of Israel (Joshua 6:2–5)? Why is this significant?

2. Describe details of the battle plan.

3. How might military experts describe the battle plan?

4. Why did Joshua follow orders so precisely?

5. Why did God order His soldiers to destroy all people in Jericho? See Deuteronomy 20:16–18.

6. Who in the city of Jericho was spared? Why? Of whom would she be an ancestor?

7. What benefits did Israel receive through this victory?

8. What consequences would they experience if they turned away from God? See Joshua 24:9–13.

Apply

For Israel at Jericho, "the battle is the Lord's." He planned it. He fought it. He won the victory. For His people.

What sorts of battles do we fight? The battle against Satan's temptations to fall into all kinds of sins? The battle for our minds over evolution, humanism, and acceptance of "alternative lifestyles"? The battle against conforming? Struggles against sinful habits, immoral thoughts, self-doubts?

As for Israel, these battles, too, are the Lord's. He fights for us! He promises to be with us at every pressure-packed moment. We do not battle Satan alone; *God* is with us. He provides strength or the means to escape temptation. We need not be embarrassed about holding to biblical teachings or values or morality; *God* will show that His Word is true and His way best. When we say no to temptation, it's *God* speaking up. And it's *God* who is with us at work, at play, and at home.

Yet God not only fights on behalf of His children. In Christ Jesus, He has already gained the victory—over Satan, over our sins, and over every other enemy. We have forgiveness for every battle lost, and we have the assurance of the final battle won through the Savior's death and resurrection.

1. What battles have you fought or are you fighting presently? How can other Christians help you?

2. What battle plan did you—or have you—developed in order to win the fight? Describe the success of your plan.

3. How does God's battle plan to defeat the enemies of the people of Israel give you comfort?

4. God battled to defeat your enemies—enemies that would lead you to death. Jesus suffered and died on the cross. When He rose from the grave, He proclaimed His victory over sin, death, and the power of the devil. How does this fact give you hope as you face enemies/battles?

5. Write a prayer of praise and thanksgiving to God for winning your battle against sin, death, and the power of Satan through His Son, Jesus Christ.

Catechism Connection

Review the First Commandment and Martin Luther's explanation in the opening for Session 6.

1. Who is God? How do Matthew 3:17; 28:19; Acts 5:3–4; 1 Corinthians 8:4; and 2 Corinthians 13:14 help you answer this question?

2. What attitude toward Himself does God demand in Joshua 5:15 and Psalm 33:8? What are some ways we display this attitude?

3. Read Matthew 22:37. Above all else, what does God require of us? If this is impossible, how can we be saved?

Send

To Do This Week

Family Connection

1. Review together the incredible events of the battle of Jericho. Ask, "How is God's work evident in the account?"

2. Develop strategies for helping one another with the battles members of your family face.

3. In your family prayers this week, thank Jesus for winning the battle for you against sin, death, and Satan. Ask God to continue to battle the forces of evil for you, and praise God for the victory He won for you in the person and work of Jesus.

Personal Reflection

1. Meditate on the words of Psalm 129. Consider the battles God has won for you through Christ Jesus.

2. Share with a friend or loved one who is experiencing trouble how God has strengthened and encouraged you as you have faced hardships.

For Next Week

Read Judges 6–7 and 13–16 in preparation for the next session.

Session 8

God Provides Victory through Judges

(Judges 6–7; 13–16)

— Gather —

Theme: History Repeats Itself

Key Point

God continues to call us to repentance through His Word, so that He might lavish upon us His grace—grace revealed in and through the person and work of Jesus.

Objectives

By the power of the Holy Spirit working through God's Word, we will

1. describe the cycle of sin, repentance, and deliverance revealed in Judges;
2. confess our sin and receive God's grace revealed in the person and work of Jesus for our forgiveness;
3. rely upon God at all times.

Opening

Read the Fifth Petition of the Lord's Prayer and Martin Luther's explanation:

Group: And forgive us our trespasses as we forgive those who trespass against us.

Leader: What does this mean?

Group: We pray in this petition that our Father in heaven would not look at our sins, or deny our prayer because of them. We are neither worthy of the things for which we pray, nor have we deserved them, but we ask that He would give them all to us by grace, for we daily sin much and surely deserve nothing but punishment. So we too will sincerely forgive and gladly do good to those who sin against us.

Introduction
1. Provide evidence of the saying "History repeats itself."

2. How does this statement describe our faith relationship with God?

In today's lesson we once again encounter the Israelites turning from God, tormented by the result of their sin, repenting and crying out to God, and receiving God's deliverance. This history repeats itself today.

Study

Reading the Text
At the death of Joshua (about the year 1375 B.C.), much of the land of Canaan had been conquered. Shares had been allotted to each tribe, and the Israelites began to settle down in their new homes. God's plan, however, was that little by little they would drive out the remaining Canaanite people and take possession of their full inheritance (Joshua 23:1–8; Exodus 23:29–33). Tragically, complacency set in. Israel became content to allow heathen nations to live among them (Judges 1:21–35). Just as God had warned (Exodus 34:11–16), Israel began to worship heathen gods.

Now God would no longer drive out the Canaanites. Instead a cycle began that would repeat itself for some three hundred years: (1) Israel would fall into idolatry, (2) God would allow an enemy to torment her, (3) Israel would repent and cry out to the Lord, (4) God would send a deliverer who would defeat the invader and judge the people for a time. But then the judge would die, Israel would revert to idolatry, and the cycle would begin again (Judges 2:11–23). The period of the judges was thus an age of chaos and spiritual bankruptcy—"everyone did as he saw fit" (21:25).

Typical of these cycles are the stories of Gideon and Samson. Each begins when Israel does "evil in the eyes of the Lord" (6:1; 13:1). From this period on, the recurring "evil" would often be worship of Baal and Asherah (Ashtoreth), the chief god and goddess of the Canaanites (6:25). Since these were deities of fertility, their worship involved lewd sexual acts and child sacrifice.

In the days of Gideon, God gave Israel over to be troubled by the Midianites and Amalekites (6:1–6). These were nomadic peoples, related to Israel, from the deserts east of the Jordan (Genesis 25:1–2; 36:15–16). They did not come as an army to conquer and hold territory. Rather, year after year, at the time of harvest, they would migrate—with families, animals, and possessions—to feed off the land of their neighbors. Not only were they as numerous as locusts (6:5), but they were as devastating to the crops and livelihood of Israel.

When Israel finally realizes her sin (6:6–10), God sends His "angel" (once again the Lord Himself, 6:12, 14) to Gideon, a man of the tribe of Manasseh (6:11–24). Though Gideon is personally insignificant (6:15), the angel rightly calls him a "mighty warrior" (6:12), for with God on his side he will surely rout the Midianites (6:16). Gideon at first is not so sure; three times he asks God for signs (6:17, 36–37, 39). Each time God graciously provides (6:18–21, 38, 40). (We should remember, of course, that God gives *us* all the assurance we need in Holy Scripture; we are not invited to ask for the kind of signs Gideon received.)

Moved by the Holy Spirit, Gideon summons his brother Israelites to war (6:34–35). The response is too good! Thirty-two thousand men turn out. Even at this, Israel will be badly outnumbered, since Midian counts 135,000 swordsmen (8:10). Yet God knows that with an army of this size Israel will still mistakenly think she has won the battle by her own might. The troops are thinned; only those truly ready to fight remain (7:1–8). Those who cup their hands and "lap the water like a dog" would still be on their feet and on the alert, while those who fall down to the ground to drink would be vulnerable. The 300 good men still enlisted are now outnumbered 450 to 1!

Three hundred soldiers are enough when the Lord fights for His people! His courage once more buoyed by a remarkable dream (7:9–15), Gideon positions his small army in three divisions around the Midianite camp (7:16–22). Each man wears his weapons but carries a trumpet and a torch concealed inside an earthenware jar. In the dark of night, just after 10 P.M. (7:19), the Israelites smash their jars, revealing the flames. They blow their trumpets and shout, "A sword for the Lord and for Gideon!" The effect is terrifying. Since ordinarily only a few members of an armed contingent would carry trumpets, these three hundred seem to herald a vast army. God throws the Midianites into confusion so that they slaughter one another. With the enemy in panicked flight, many additional Israelites—no doubt including some of the soldiers previously released—complete the rout (7:23–25).

By the days of Samson, a new adversary had arisen. The Philistines, who would be Israel's chief enemy in the years to come, were an extremely warlike people. Like Israel, they were relative newcomers to the land and, though living along the Mediterranean coast, were always looking to expand their territory. They forged tools and weapons of iron, giving them a decided advantage over the Israelites, who for the most part still used bronze (1 Samuel 13:19–22). The whole land of Canaan eventually came to be named after them: Palestine.

When Israel deserts the Lord, she is powerless against this enemy. Yet, as always, God remains faithful to His people. Once more the angel of the Lord appears with wonderful news: A childless couple of the tribe of Dan, Manoah and his wife, will have a son who will "begin" to deliver Israel (Judges 13:5). Let him be warned, though: From the womb he is set apart by the vow of a Nazirite (Numbers 6:2–5). For most, this vow is temporary. Samson, however, is *never* to drink alcohol or to have his hair cut (Judges 13:7).

Samson may not be an unusually large or muscular man. To the contrary, his might is a special gift of the Holy Spirit, who comes upon him at crucial moments (Judges 13:25; 14:6, 19; 15:14). In fact, the Lord works in spite of human weakness, specifically Samson's moral and spiritual weakness. The Lord first brings Samson into conflict with the Philistines as a result of Samson's sinful choice of a wife (14:1–4). Earlier, God had forbidden his people to intermarry with their unbelieving neighbors (Deuteronomy 7:3–4). Nevertheless, God uses the situation to inflict casualties on Israel's enemy (14:19; 15:3–8, 14–16).

Sadly, Samson loses sight both of his divinely appointed mission and of the Source of his strength (16:1–22). He begins to feel that the power is *his*, that he can rescue himself from foolish risks—to say nothing of immoral entanglements (16:1, 4). Significantly, during these last incidents of Samson's life, the Spirit of the Lord is not mentioned as coming upon him. Believing *himself* to be invincible, he finally gives in to Delilah's seduction, knowing full well that she has betrayed him three times already.

The sins of God's people give His enemies occasion to blaspheme (16:23–24; 2 Samuel 12:14). At last, however, Samson is repentant. Helpless, blind, depending on a young boy to lead him, he understands that his strength must come from God. Once more he is willing to devote himself to his mission. His death deals a serious blow to the Philistines; three thousand people and all of their leading nobles are killed (Judges 16:25–31). It is only a "beginning" of deliverance. God surely desired to do much more through His champion. Yet, Samson, like Gideon, is remembered in the "Faith Hall of Fame" (Hebrews 11).

Discussing the Text

1. How did complacency toward the Canaanites ultimately threaten the relationship of the Israelites with God?

2. Describe the steps in the cycle of sin and repentance. See Judges 2:16–19.

3. How was the cycle evident in the story of Gideon?

4. How was the cycle evident in the story of Samson?

5. In spite of the people's faithlessness, how did God remain faithful to His people?

6. How does God's action relate to His promise to Abraham in Genesis 15:5?

Apply

At least four applications of these stories—two of Law and two of Gospel—may be important to us. Of the Law: (1) The whole period of the judges is a warning against forgetting the grace and blessings of God. Given a lavish homeland they had not tilled, given victory after victory, the Israelites quickly turned away from the One who had blessed them. The consequences were painful, but not nearly as devastating as the eternal ones for all who reject their eternal Savior. (2) Samson is a tragic illustration of those who rely on themselves rather than on the Lord. Our strength never really lies in ourselves. On our own we are helpless. We are always dependent on God. Trusting in Him, "we are more than conquerors" (Romans 8:37).

Of the Gospel: (3) The cycles of the judges, on the other hand, again and again reveal God's faithfulness. Israel's unbelief seems ample grounds to reject the nation forever. Instead, God's forgiveness always becomes the last word. "Where sin increased, grace increased all the more" (Romans 5:20). Another delivery and another and another, until, finally, the Ultimate Deliverer, Christ Jesus, would come. (4) The Lord triumphs with a few as easily as with many. When Gideon stood with 300 against thousands, when Samson fought all alone, they were never really outnumbered. God was with them. When we feel alone or helpless, we may always trust that the Lord is with us at all times. Our Savior's promise is sure (Matthew 28:20).

1. "History repeats itself." How is this evident in the cycle of sin and repentance throughout history? today?

2. In spite of people's unbelief and lack of faith, God continues to invite sinful people to come to Him through His Word. How does this invitation demonstrate God's love and faithfulness?

3. Compare the cycle described in Judges to the cycle described in James 1:13–15. On our own we are unable to stop the cycle of destruction. But God in His love for us, "when we were still powerless" (Romans 5:6), sent Jesus to die for us. How does God's love for us break the cycle?

4. Read Luke 7:37–38, 44–50. Note the way a sinful woman responded to the love of Jesus. What are some ways we respond to His love?

5. Write a brief prayer thanking God for continuing to remain faithful to us in spite of our lack of trust. Be prepared to share the prayer for the closing activity.

Catechism Connection

Examine the Fifth Petition and Martin Luther's explanation in the opening for this session.

1. What do we confess when we pray this petition? Why is it important to make this confession? See Psalm 130:3–4.

2. What does it show when we forgive others?

Send

To Do This Week

Family Connection

1. As you begin your devotions each day, ask each family member to flex his or her muscles. Say, "The same God who gave strength to Samson also gives us the power to do great things for Him."

2. Ask, "How can God's love for us in Jesus stop our history of sin from repeating itself?"

3. Pray together, thanking God for the deliverance He has provided you through faith in Jesus from sin, death, and the power of the devil.

Personal Reflection

1. Reread James 1:13–15. Consider how the cycle described by James is evident at times in your life.

2. Confess your sinful disobedience to God, trusting that "when we were still powerless, Christ died for the ungodly."

3. Commit yourself to sharing the cycle of God's love in your life with a friend and/or loved one who hasn't experienced the magnitude of God's love in Christ.

For Next Week

Read the Book of Ruth in preparation for the next class session.

Session 9

God Blesses Ruth

(The Book of Ruth)

Gather

Theme: Devoted

Key Point

Jesus' selfless love for us motivates us to respond in love for others.

Objectives

By the power of the Holy Spirit working through God's Word, we will

1. describe the devotion of Ruth and Boaz;
2. describe God's devotion to us revealed in His Son's life, death, and resurrection;
3. demonstrate selfless love to others in response to God's love for us.

Opening

Read the Fourth Commandment and Martin Luther's explanation:

Group: Honor your father and your mother.
Leader: What does this mean?
Group: We should fear and love God so that we do not despise or anger our parents and other authorities, but honor them, serve and obey them, love and cherish them.

Introduction

1. "I am devoted to . . ." Finish this sentence starter with as many different responses as possible.

2. How do you demonstrate devotion?

3. Who is devoted to you? How do you know this?

In our lesson for today we witness selfless devotion between Ruth and Boaz—the great-grandparents of David and ancestors of Jesus. God in Christ showered us with selfless devotion as Jesus went to the cross so that we might inherit eternal life.

Study

Reading the Text

Amid the spiritual decadence of the period of the Judges, the story of Ruth comes as welcome refreshment. God continues to accomplish His will through chosen individuals, even though the nation of Israel seems to go its own wicked way. Through the faithfulness of Ruth, Naomi, and Boaz, God gives a vivid picture of the future Redeemer, Jesus Christ. At the same time, God makes the next necessary arrangements toward the Savior's birth into the world.

Most of the story is set in Bethlehem, the first connection between the ancient village and the promise of the Messiah (see also Micah 5:2). Though the "house of bread," Bethlehem is ravaged by a famine. Naomi and her family are forced to seek a living in Moab, Israel's neighbor to the southeast, a move of up to 100 miles (Ruth 1:1–2).

After 10 years, prosperity has returned to Israel. Yet Naomi (whose name means "pleasant") is herself empty, having lost her husband and two sons (1:3–6). She now prefers to be called Mara, or "bitter" (1:20–21). She blesses her Moabite daughters-in-law in the name of the Lord (1:9), fully expecting them to remain in their homeland as Naomi returns to hers. She has nothing to offer them. God's law of "levirate marriage" would normally have provided for the young widows by giving Naomi's other sons as husbands (Deuteronomy 25:5–10). But Naomi is childless and poor (1:11–13).

Ruth's decision to go with Naomi was an expression of faith in the God of Israel. Orpah returned "to her people and her gods" (1:15), but Ruth realized that her salvation—both earthly and eternal—lay in becoming one of Yahweh's people. This motivated her tender loyalty to Naomi, even at the prospect of life-long widowhood in a strange land (1:16–18).

Ruth's faithfulness is evident as she supports her aging mother-in-law (Ruth 2). God had made provision for the poor by commanding landowners to leave behind a portion of their crops to be picked up by the needy (Deuteronomy 24:19–22). Clearly He was making special provision for Ruth, because the field in which she "happened" to glean belonged to Boaz (2:3).

Now Boaz was in a unique position to help Ruth and Naomi. Not only was he God-fearing and wealthy, he was also a close relative of Naomi's late husband (2:1, 20). This made him a potential "kinsman-redeemer." Again under the law of levirate marriage, a close relative had the duty of "redeeming" the widow—making her his own wife—and maintaining the family line of the deceased. With this obligation might come the privilege of redeeming also the inheritance of the dead relative. There might, of course, be a price to pay.

Seeing the potential, Naomi advises Ruth to petition Boaz (3:1–5). Her request comes as a humble plea for help: "Spread the corner of your garment over me" (3:9)—just as God takes the helpless "under His wings" (2:12). Following a custom of the day, Ruth literally uncovered Boaz's feet, a symbolic request for marriage. Likewise literally, he invited her to lie at his feet until morning, as a token that he would not hurt her and that he was not spurning her request.

One formality had first to be resolved (4:1–12). Another relative was closer than Boaz and thus had first right to redeem. Meeting the next morning at the city gate (the usual seat of government and business), Boaz apprised this relative of the situation. The man was eager to exercise the *privilege* of redeeming property belonging to Naomi. However, when Boaz informed him that there was an accompanying *duty* as well—to marry the widow and raise up an heir for the deceased—the man balked. He knew that if he were to father an heir for the deceased and then die without a son of his own, his own estate would pass to Naomi's family.

By contrast, Boaz was more than willing to pay the necessary price and take the necessary risks to care for Ruth (4:13–22). Far from losing his estate, Boaz is ever remembered. For he and Ruth became the great-grandparents of David and, centuries later, ancestors of the great Redeemer, Jesus. In the end, all is well. Naomi is full once more (4:14–17). Israel has hope of better days under a noble king (4:22). And Ruth, a woman, a foreigner, takes her place in the lineage of the Savior (Matthew 1:5–16).

Discussing the Text

1. What events occurred that caused Naomi to prefer being called Mara? See Ruth 1:1–5, 20–21.

2. Why did Ruth decide to go with Naomi (1:10, 16–17)?

3. Why was Boaz in the unique position to help Ruth and Naomi (2:1, 20)?

4. Describe the role of the kinsman-redeemer.

5. What caused the other relative not to exercise his privilege of becoming Naomi's kinsman-redeemer (4:4–6)?

6. What impresses you most about the actions of God in this account?

Apply

Ruth and Boaz each present a useful application. Ruth is a beautiful example of love that comes from faith. She is first and foremost a believer in the true God (1:16). She trusts that God will be with her even in loneliness and poverty. She believes that life in Him, come what may, will be more blessed than anything she might have without Him. As a result, she is devoted to her mother-in-law (1:14), selfless and industrious (2:2), humble (2:10, 13), and morally upright (3:10–11). Faith in Christ brings that sort of response from us as well. As we recall the love God has for us, our lives, too, will reflect, however imperfectly, the qualities of Ruth.

Boaz, meanwhile, is an active illustration of Christ Himself. Jesus is the ultimate Kinsman-Redeemer. Like Boaz, Jesus truly became our relative, our Brother. Jesus willingly left His own inheritance, the glory of heaven, to take ours, the suffering and death and hell that we had earned by our sin. And, most dramatically, Jesus paid the awful price to redeem us, to buy us back from sin, death, and the power of the devil. Jesus redeemed us with His lifeblood (1 Peter 1:18–19). As we see Boaz caring for Ruth and taking her in, we may also know that Jesus has done this for us—"not with gold or silver, but with His holy, precious blood and with His innocent suffering and death."

1. What was the significance of Ruth, a foreigner, taking her place in the lineage of Jesus? See Acts 10:34–35.

2. What qualities did Ruth possess that demonstrated her faith in the one true God?

3. Compare Boaz's action on behalf of Naomi to the action of Jesus on our behalf. See 1 Peter 1:18–19.

4. How does God's love for us in Christ motivate us to demonstrate devotion to others? What words and actions demonstrate your devotion to others?

Catechism Connection

Examine the Fourth Commandment and Martin Luther's explanation in the opening for this session.

1. How do Ruth's actions demonstrate obedience to Proverbs 23:22?

2. Read 1 Timothy 5:4. What are some ways we can put these instructions into practice?

3. Read Acts 5:29. When must we disobey earthly authorities?

Send

To Do This Week

Family Connection

1. List ways to show devotion to one another. For one week put a check mark after an item on the list when someone notices a family member showing devotion in that way.

2. Ask, "How can we demonstrate devotion to one another?" Make a list of things you can do to demonstrate devotion to the members of your family.

3. Compare devotion to selfishness. What are the characteristics of a person who is selfish? What are the characteristics of a person who is devoted?

4. Review how Jesus was the "Kinsman-Redeemer" of each member of your family. Discuss how Jesus began this work at your Baptism.

Personal Reflection

1. Reread Ruth and underline or list the characteristics of a person who demonstrates devotion. Consider your devotion to others. What additional things could you say or do to demonstrate devotion to others?

2. Meditate on the devotion God demonstrated to you through His only Son's death on the cross.

3. Share devotion with a friend or loved one. Tell him or her the reason for your devotion—devotion that flows from the love of God in Christ Jesus.

For Next Week

Read 1 Samuel 1:1–2:11 and 3:1–21 in preparation for the next lesson.

Session 10

God Calls Samuel

(1 Samuel 1:1–2:11; 3:1–21)

Gather

Theme: Overlooked, Unimportant, and Insecure

Key Point

God has empowered us with His gifts so that we might share the worth He won for us in Christ Jesus with all people, so that they, too, might know how precious they are to Him.

Objectives

By the power of the Holy Spirit working through God's Word, we will
1. describe how God can and does use the seemingly most insignificant people to accomplish His will and purpose;
2. affirm the worth God has provided to us through His Son's death;
3. seek new ways to share the worth God has provided us through Jesus with those who do not know Him.

Opening

Read the Introduction to the Lord's Prayer and Martin Luther's explanation.

Group: Our Father who art in heaven.

Leader: What does this mean?

Group: With these words God tenderly invites us to believe that He is our true Father and that we are His true children, so that with all boldness and confidence we may ask Him as dear children ask their dear father.

Introduction

1. Describe a time when you have felt overlooked, unimportant, or insecure. What caused you to feel this way?

2. "If you had been the only person on earth, Jesus would have died for you." Respond to this statement.

In today's lesson God uses those the world would consider insignificant to move forward His grand plan for salvation through Jesus Christ. He continues to use those today whom the world would consider insignificant to share His message of salvation.

Study

Reading the Text

Samuel was the miracle child of Elkanah and one of his two wives, Hannah. Although an Ephraimite (1 Samuel 1:1), Elkanah was in fact of the tribe of Levi, his family having received its inheritance within the territory of Ephraim. (See 1 Chronicles 6:16–28 and Joshua 21:1–3, 20–21, 41.) Already in this respect God's hand is evident, since Samuel would function as a priest, and the priesthood was to come exclusively from Levi.

Elkanah's polygamy brought on difficulties for his home (1 Samuel 1:2–8). Hannah had no child, and her rival seemed to relish bringing up the fact. For a Hebrew woman, this was particularly painful; childlessness was stigmatized as rejection by God. Despite Elkanah's special kindness (1 Samuel 1:5, 8), Hannah grieved deeply.

Each year Elkanah and his family would travel to Shiloh to sacrifice at the tabernacle (Exodus 23:14–17; Luke 2:41). Centrally located for all Israel, also within the inheritance of Ephraim, Shiloh became the permanent home of the "tent of meeting" once Israel had entered Canaan (Joshua 18:1; but see also 1 Samuel 4:1–11 and Psalm 78:54–61). Permanent structures, including sleeping quarters, now apparently supplemented the tabernacle complex, so that it could be called a "temple" (1 Samuel 1:9; 3:2–3, 15). The first "real" temple, to be built by Solomon, was still more than a century in the future.

On one of their trips to Shiloh, Hannah poured out her heart to the Lord. She promised God that if He would give her a son, she would dedicate the child to His service (1:9–18). Like Samson, he would be a Nazirite for life (Numbers 6:2–5). The spiritual condition in Israel must have been so bad that Eli, the high priest, at first assumed Hannah was intoxicated. His quick rebuke gave way to a blessing. He sent Hannah to her home with hope that God would answer her prayer. Hannah's outlook on life was instantly transformed (1:18).

God indeed heard and answered her prayer. Appropriately, Hannah named her baby Samuel ("heard of God"). Children were often nursed for three years or more in ancient Israel; but as soon as Samuel was weaned, Hannah kept her vow. The little boy was brought to the tabernacle to serve God. Samuel grew up assisting Eli (1:19–28). His parents visited each year and brought him a new robe (2:19). Doubtless they also brought lavish affection and holy pride!

For her part, Hannah was overjoyed. Her prayer of thanksgiving—a hymn—radiated the heartfelt gratitude of one who had been lifted from the depths to the heights (2:1–10). It is sometimes called "The Magnificat of the Old Testament" because it so parallels the song of Mary before the birth of Jesus ("My soul magnifies the Lord," Luke 1:46–55). Later she had even more to sing about: God gave her five more children (2:20–21).

God's plan for Samuel was, however, only beginning. Perhaps around the boy's twelfth year, the Lord appeared to Samuel for the first time (3:1–18). Through his parents and his teacher, Eli, Samuel already knew the Lord as Savior. To this point, though, God had revealed no specific word to him. In fact, such words or visions of the Lord were rare, even to Eli, Israel's priest (3:1).

The call comes in the hours approaching dawn, since the lamp of the Lord was soon to be renewed (3:3; Leviticus 24:2–4). Quite naturally, Samuel assumes the voice to be Eli's, and his prompt response—three times—is a highlight of the story. Samuel is a faithful servant, listening carefully to the voice. Finally Eli realizes that it is the Lord who is calling the boy. Once more Samuel is obedient: when this time the Lord "[comes] and [stands]" before him, Samuel answers, "Speak, for Your servant is listening" (3:10).

The message God reveals to Samuel is devastating (3:11–14). Some time before, God had pronounced to Eli himself judgment for indulging the wickedness of his sons (2:12–17, 22, 27–36). Now Samuel hears the same sad news about his mentor. Eli takes it well enough (3:15–18). He knows that God's punishment is deserved. But more important, he understands—as all Israel soon will—that God has raised up a new judge and prophet (3:19–21). Over the next decades, Samuel will be God's mouthpiece to direct the nation toward a more excellent way.

Discussing the Text

1. Read 1 Samuel 1:1–6. Why did Hannah feel overlooked and unimportant? See also Psalm 128:3.

2. What did Hannah promise to the Lord if He would give her a son (1 Samuel 1:11)? What is the significance of this promise?

3. Compare Hannah's prayer of thanksgiving (2:1–10) to the song of Mary before the birth of Jesus (Luke 1:46–55).

4. Explain the unique characteristics of Samuel's call by God. (1 Samuel 3:1–14).

5. Why was the message that God revealed to Samuel devastating to Eli?

6. What does God's choosing Samuel over the sons of Eli say about God's love for His people?

Apply

The primary applications of the lesson are not the exemplary behavior of the human characters—Hannah with her humble prayer, Samuel with his obedience. Rather, the real point of the story is God's rich grace showered upon ordinary, unworthy, and insignificant people. Hannah is a woman who feels desolate. Samuel is just a little boy. But God blesses them and uses them. In fact, He lifts them up to become great names for thousands of years to come. Hannah's song actually expresses the point of the Books of Samuel: Israel, a helpless and insignificant collection of rabble under the judges, will become a world power under King David, himself a man whom God lifted to the throne from tending sheep (2 Samuel 7:8–16).

We may sometimes feel overlooked, unimportant, and insecure. The marvelous message of these stories is that God considers us very important. He knows each of us. He cares about us. He has revealed the depth of His love by giving His Son to die for the sins of the world. In Christ, each person is precious in God's sight. He will lift us up and use us for His grand design to bring salvation to the ends of the earth.

1. How does God use the insignificant and unworthy of this world?

2. How does the message of this story relate to your life?

3. How has and will God use you for service to Him?

4. How does the love of God demonstrated in the person and work of Jesus give you hope and comfort when you feel over-looked, unimportant, or insecure?

5. What might you say to a person who indicates that she/he feels overlooked, unimportant, or insecure?

Catechism Connection

Examine the Introduction to the Lord's Prayer and Martin Luther's explanation in the opening for this session.

1. Read Romans 8:15–16. Why may we address God as *Father*?

2. What good news about God the Father do you find in 1 John 3:1 and Psalm 103:13?

3. At times our troubles may overwhelm us so much that we find it difficult to pray with confidence. What assurance for such times do you find in Romans 8:26–28?

Send

To Do This Week

Family Connection

1. Compare your family to the families described in the Bible lesson.

2. Have each person in your family share how the other members of your family are important.

3. Speak the words of Hannah's song of thanksgiving before or after each meal this week.

4. Together, write a family song of thanksgiving.

Personal Reflection

1. Reflect on the magnitude of God's love for you in Jesus.

2. Be a friend to someone who may feel overlooked, unimportant, or insecure.

3. Meditate on the words of Hannah's song of thanksgiving and Mary's song of praise.

For Next Week

Read 1 Samuel 3 and 8–11 in preparation for the next session.

Session 11

God Gives Leaders to Israel

(1 Samuel 3; 8–11)

--- **Gather** ---

Theme: Like All the Others

Key Point

By the power of the Holy Spirit working through the Gospel, God transforms our lives so that we desire to conform to His will.

Objectives

By the power of the Holy Spirit working through God's Word, we will
1. explain how the desire of Israel to have a king like all the other nations was rebellion against God;
2. confess our own desires to conform to this world even if it means denying or disregarding God's will for us;
3. demonstrate desire to conform to God's will for our lives as we are motivated by the forgiveness Jesus won for us on the cross.

Opening

Read responsively parts 1 and 4 of "The Sacrament of Holy Baptism" from Luther's Small Catechism.

Leader: What is Baptism?

Group: Baptism is not just plain water, but it is the water included in God's command and combined with God's word.

Leader: Which is that word of God?

Group: Christ our Lord says in the last chapter of Matthew: "Therefore go and make disciples of all nations, baptizing them in the name of the Father and of the Son and of the Holy Spirit." [Matthew 28:19]

Leader: What does such baptizing with water indicate?

Group: It indicates that the Old Adam in us should by daily contrition and repentance be drowned and die with all sins and evil desires, and that a new man should daily emerge and arise to live before God in righteousness and purity forever.

Leader: Where is this written?

Group: St. Paul writes in Romans chapter six: "We were therefore buried with Him through baptism into death in order that, just as Christ was raised from the dead through the glory of the Father, we too may live a new life." [Romans 6:4]

Introduction

We sometimes accuse teenagers of caving in to peer pressure in order to be like others. But, if honest, we must confess that we as adults try to be like others, too.

1. How do our thoughts, words, and actions often reflect our desire to be like others?

2. What danger might we encounter if, as we try to be like others, we forget or lose sight of how we belong to God through Baptism ?

In today's lesson the Israelites demand to have a king like all the other nations. This demand is in direct conflict with God's desires. God provides to Saul everything he needs to be Israel's king. God continues to be in control despite His people's rejection.

Study

Reading the Text

For commentary on 1 Samuel 3, see Session 10.

"Give us a king like all the other nations!"

Samuel is old and his sons unfit to lead Israel. It is time for a change—but a change to what? Since the day of deliverance from slavery in Egypt, Israel has had only one King: the Lord. Moses, Joshua and the judges were God's mouthpieces; yet they were never invested with the rights of royalty. Now, however, the elders of Israel come to Samuel, asking for a human king (1 Samuel 8:1–5). What will Samuel say?

In truth, God had always planned to give Israel a king. He had promised that kings would descend from Abraham and Sarah (Genesis 17:6, 16). A scepter had been prophesied for Judah and Israel (Genesis 49:10; Numbers 24:17). Hannah had foreseen a powerful monarchy (1 Samuel 2:10). God had even anticipated the people asking for a king (Deuteronomy 17:14–15). A human king was a key part of God's purpose for Israel, because an earthly king would serve as a living illustration of the future messianic King.

Nevertheless, the elders' request troubled Samuel (1 Samuel 8:6–9). The desire for a king was not an issue. Rather, the reason for wanting a king was the problem. God's people wanted to be "like all the other nations" (8:20). They believed that their neighbors' human kings provided greater protection from enemies than they had experienced in the past. This was a direct rejection of the Lord, for God had always been their Protector. (The irony is that Israel wanted to be like the very kingdoms the Lord had subdued!) Moreover, wanting to be like the other nations was a blatant repudiation of the covenant God had established with them at Mount Sinai. God had set them apart to be *different*—to be a unique, holy nation (Exodus 19:4–6).

Thus God wished to provide a king, but of a certain kind—one who would be a "man after His own heart" (1 Samuel 13:14). The people were asking for a very different sort of king—a mighty warrior, an impressive man. Samuel plainly warned the people of the consequences: Their sort of king would draft their sons, take their daughters, and tax them heavily (8:10–18; 1 Kings 12:12–14).

God's king, by contrast, was to be a modest servant, a follower of God's Word and ways (Deuteronomy 17:14–20; 1 Samuel 10:25).

Samuel reported Israel's demands to the Lord, and the Lord consented. The people would have a king—their kind of king (8:19–22). Still, the Lord would give that man everything he needed to be *God's* king. God would change his heart (10:6, 9) to be more like His own. As long as he continued to follow the word of the Lord, God would prosper his reign.

The man who meets the people's expectations is Saul. He comes from a warrior family (9:1). He is as handsome as any man in the land and a full head taller (9:2). Even so, his success will depend solely on God's help. He comes from Israel's smallest tribe, Benjamin, a tribe nearly destroyed by civil war (Judges 20–21). He is at first highly indecisive (1 Samuel 9:3–10) and painfully shy (10:20–22). He is in no position to gather a following (10:26–27).

Samuel, therefore, gives Saul encouragement from the Lord. He honors Saul at a banquet (9:11–24). He spends hours in private instruction with Saul (9:25). He anoints Saul, pouring olive oil over his head as a symbol that Saul has been chosen by the Lord and equipped for this special task (9:26–10:1; also Leviticus 8:10–12). He gives Saul three convincing signs that God will be with him (10:2–13).

Finally, Samuel assembles all Israel at Mizpah to publicly identify the new king (10:17–25). Saul is chosen by random lot, perhaps by using the Urim and Thummim, sacred lots kept by the high priest for inquiring of the Lord (Exodus 28:30). In this way, God undeniably confirms Saul's selection for all—including Saul himself—to see.

Now what to do? Saul actually goes back to working his father's fields ... until a crisis arises (1 Samuel 11:1–13). By the power of God's Spirit (11:6), Saul is equal to the challenge, and Israel is ready to follow its new king. A huge army—330,000 volunteers—answers the call to arms, and God brings swift victory. Saul is off to a good start as ruler of God's people.

Samuel will not, however, let the Israelites forget who has really secured the triumph. He summons the people to Gilgal, Israel's first place of worship in Canaan (Joshua 4:19–20; 5:10), to "reaffirm the kingship" (1 Samuel 11:14–15). Only secondarily do the ceremonies confirm Saul as king; the peace offerings actually reaffirm the kingship of the Lord. Let Saul and all Israel remember that the nation will be blessed by its monarchy only as long as God remains on the throne.

Discussing the Text

1. Why was Samuel troubled by the elders' request for a king? Read 1 Samuel 8:1–8. Why was Israel's desire for a king ironic?

2. The Israelites wanted a king "like all the other nations." How did God demonstrate His love for the Israelites by providing "a man after His own heart"?

3. God referred to David as "a man after His own heart" (13:14). At the beginning of Saul's reign, why may we use the same phrase to describe him? See 10:6, 9.

4. Read 1 Samuel 9:25–10:13. How did Samuel prepare Saul to become the king of Israel?

5. How did Samuel remind the people that their real king was God Himself? See 1 Samuel 10:17, 25, and 11:12–15.

Apply

A simple truth shines through this lesson: God rules. We should never place our trust in anyone else. "You shall have no other gods before Me." No other human being—close friend, peer, parent, teacher—is the ultimate authority or the ultimate source of help. Nor can we expect to be in final control of our own lives.

On the other hand, this also means that we are citizens of a truly awesome Kingdom. With God as our King, we may always be certain of justice, kindness, and freedom. We may be sure that no spiritual enemy can conquer us. We may even look forward to reigning with Him, as kings under the King of kings, Jesus Christ (Revelation 17:14); Christ's death and resurrection bestow on us a crown of eternal life (Revelation 2:10).

1. How do we at times demonstrate in our lives that we want to be like all the others, even when being like all the others rejects God's will for our lives? How does this reject God's First Commandment?

2. In spite of our sinful rejection, through His Word God continues to offer His love and forgiveness through faith in Christ Jesus. What comfort does this truth provide you?

3. God is our King. What is the significance of this statement, considering what we have learned in the lesson for today?

4. Read 2 Corinthians 3:7–9, 17–18. How do we become instruments for use in God's service?

Catechism Connection

Examine the Catechism sections about Baptism in the opening for this session.

1. Read Acts 2:38–39. When does an infant receive the Spirit of God?

2. In what ways do Matthew 28:19–20 and Luke 18:15–17 authenticate the practice of infant baptism?

3. How does your Baptism remain important throughout

your life? See, for example, 1 Corinthians 6:9–11.

Send

To Do This Week

Family Connection

1. Review the events of the Bible story. Discuss how the people's desire demonstrated rebellion against God. Ask, "How did God respond to His people in spite of their rebellion?"

2. Read Romans 5:6–11. Ask, "How did God respond to us in spite of our rebellion?"

3. Talk together about the time when each family member became a member of God's family.

4. Motivated by God's love, how might our family members support each other when we recognize that someone in the family makes someone or something more important than God?

Personal Reflection

1. Confess your sinful desires to be like all the others, even when it means rejecting God.

2. Meditate on the magnitude of God's love revealed in the words of Romans 5:6–11.

3. Write the words *God is my King* on a note card. Place it in a conspicuous place, where you will see it often.

For Next Week

Read 1 Samuel 13:1–15 and 15:1–17:54 in preparation for the next session.

Session 12

God Chooses David

(1 Samuel 13:1–15; 15:1–17:54)

— Gather —

Theme: Against All Odds

Key Point

God is with us at all times, ready to fight against all odds we may encounter.

Objectives

By the power of the Holy Spirit working through God's Word, we will

1. describe how God enabled David to be victorious against all odds;
2. confess how we, by taking matters into our own hands, demonstrate a lack of trust in God and His ability to work all things for our good;
3. rely upon God, who cared so much about us that He willingly sent His only Son to suffer and die on the cross for our sins.

Opening

Read responsively parts 2 and 3 of "The Sacrament of Holy Baptism" from Luther's Small Catechism.

Leader: What benefits does Baptism give?

Group: It works forgiveness of sins, rescues from death and the devil, and gives eternal salvation to all who believe this, as the words and promises of God declare.

Leader: Which are these words and promises of God?

Group: Christ our Lord says in the last chapter of Mark: "Whoever believes and is baptized will be saved, but whoever does not believe will be condemned." [Mark 16:16]

Leader: How can water do such great things?

Men: Certainly not just water, but the word of God in and with the water does these things, along with the faith which trusts this word of God in the water. For without God's word the water is plain water and no Baptism.

Women: But with the word of God it is a Baptism, that is, a life-giving water, rich in grace, and a washing of the new birth in the Holy Spirit, as St. Paul says in Titus, chapter three:

All: "He saved us through the washing of rebirth and renewal by the Holy Spirit, whom He poured out on us generously through Jesus Christ our Savior, so that, having been justified by His grace, we might become heirs having the hope of eternal life. This is a trustworthy saying." [Titus 3:5–8]

Introduction

1. Complete one or more of the following sentence starters:
Against all odds, we …

Against all odds, they …

Against all odds, he/she …

Against all odds, I …

2. What do the endings to the sentence starters have in common?

3. Now complete the following sentence starter with as many endings as possible:

Against all odds, God in Christ …

Today we learn how God provides a new king for the people of Israel to replace the corrupt King Saul. We witness God's guidance, protection, and power as He works for the people of Israel and His chosen replacement for Saul, David, against all odds.

Study

Reading the Text

While Israel had her own sinful reasons for demanding a king, God always had one purpose in planning the monarchy: Israel's human king was to prefigure the great King of the Jews, Jesus. A man could be God's king in Israel only as long as he reflected—however imperfectly—God's purpose. Sadly, Saul proved inadequate. God then raised up the king from whom the Messiah would descend: David, son of Jesse. In the fullness of time, David's "son," Jesus, would be born the King of the Jews.

Saul's failure as God's man is exemplified in two events. A minor victory over the Philistines brought major reprisal (13:1–5). The enemy invaded Israel with the largest force it had yet assembled. Saul retreated to Gilgal, near the Jordan River, where Samuel had promised to meet him in seven days (10:8). Samuel would offer sacrifices and bring further instructions from the Lord. But Saul panicked. His small army was growing smaller with desertions (13:6–7). Samuel was nowhere in sight. So on the seventh day, Saul offered the sacrifices himself—moments before Samuel arrived (13:8–14).

Saul's sin may seem trivial. But in fact, his actions demonstrated faithlessness: Saul took matters into his own hands, rather than waiting for God. Saul was arrogant: Only priests could offer sacrifices, and even the king could not seize powers God had not given. Saul was spiritually blind: He believed the sacrifice would magically acquire God's favor, even when the sacrifice was made in disobedience and apart from faith. Such behavior could never illustrate the messianic King. Samuel immediately pronounced God's judgment: Saul's family would not continue to rule after him. A new man, "a man after God's own heart," would succeed Saul (13:14).

Saul's second failure (15:1–35) brought an even stiffer sentence. Not only would Saul's line not continue on the throne, but Saul himself was now rejected as king. Amalek, the first enemy to trouble Israel after the Exodus (Exodus 17:8–16), had long been marked by the Lord for annihilation. Saul, therefore, was expressly sent on a holy mission to carry out God's curse, to kill every human and animal of the Amalekites. That he overruled God's command by sparing their king and the best of their flocks was bad enough. But when confronted by Samuel, he first lied (1 Samuel 15:13), then misled (15:15), then tried to shift the blame for his actions (15:20–21). Even when forced to "confess," he tried to excuse himself (15:24).

Saul had indeed become exactly what Israel had asked for—a king "such as all the other nations [had]" (8:5). He went his own way and exalted himself (15:12). He was no longer *God's* king. Saul's reign was, therefore, over. Though he would continue to rule visibly, Saul was powerless and ineffective.

After a period of mourning, Samuel is sent by the Lord to anoint a new king (16:1–13). How remarkably this one will foreshadow the Messiah! He comes from Bethlehem. He is not a tall, handsome warrior (cf. 1 Samuel 10:23–24), but a man whose heart is with the Lord. David comes in from tending sheep. His favorite words and images are those of the shepherd (Psalm 23; 1 Samuel 17:34–37, 40; 2 Samuel 7:8). David is a preview of Jesus, the Good Shepherd who lays down His life for the sheep (John 10:11). From the moment of his anointing, David is filled with the Holy Spirit (compare Acts 10:38; the Hebrew word for *anointed* is "Messiah" (Psalm 2:2; 45:7).

The other familiar image of David is the youth playing his harp. Musical talent gives David his first exposure to the duties of monarchy (1 Samuel 16:14–23). Saul is now troubled by "an evil spirit from the Lord" (16:14–16, 23; 18:10; 19:9). David's soothing music and his inspired words from God (his lyrics, the Psalms) are Saul's deliverance.

It is perhaps 15 years before David actually assumes the throne (2 Samuel 5:4). But his term as God's man for Israel begins almost immediately with an epic victory (1 Samuel 17:1–54). Goliath is a terrifying figure—nearly ten-feet tall (17:4). His armor weighs as much as most of his opponents— over 150 pounds (17:5). He carries a spear with a *head* heavier than a bowling ball—15 to 20 pounds (17:7). No one in the Israelite army dares to do battle against the giant. Clearly Saul, the king in whom Israel put her trust, tall and mighty though he is, is no match for Goliath. Without the Lord, they are *all* helpless.

Yet with God, even an inexperienced, lightly armed boy can topple the champion. Just as he will later inspire the whole nation, David brings a new spirit to the camp (17:26–30). Predictably, his oldest brother, Eliab, takes offense at his little brother's bold talk. But as David goes from one soldier to another, his question about the promised rewards is probably intended to spur one of them to take courage. "How," David asks, "could this heathen hope to stand when he has defied the armies of the living God? He should be easy prey!" (paraphrase).

A stirring confrontation! A huge man, fully outfitted for battle, against a shepherd with a staff, a sling, and five smooth stones. It is a mismatch, for a sword and spear and javelin can never contend with the Lord of hosts! One stone is all David needs. God directs it; Goliath falls. The battle belongs to the Lord!

Discussing the Text

1. What was God's one purpose in planning the monarchy for Israel?

2. What two events (1 Samuel 13:1–13; 15:1–11) exemplify Saul's failure as God's man?

3. How had Saul become exactly what Israel had asked for—a king "such as all the other nations have"?

4. How is David a preview of Jesus? See 16:11–13.

5. How did David's killing of Goliath (17:1–51) demonstrate that the battle belongs to the Lord?

Apply

Saul's decline warns against pride, empty works, and reliance on self rather than on the Lord. David is a model of faith. God's defeat of Goliath reminds that "If God is for us, who can be against us?" (Romans 8:31).

The overriding application, though, is to see in David a portrait of Christ. Each new description of David actually pictures Jesus. Jesus is the Shepherd who feeds His people, protects them, and carries them in His arms. Jesus is the One whose voice (in His Word and Supper) soothes their spirits and drives away their fears. Jesus is the mighty Champion who, by His death and resurrection, has defeated the devil and given us eternal life. In Him we have the courage to face challenges. Jesus is the King who orders every day for our good. David's real importance for us—and even for the Old Testament people—is that David introduces us to David's greater Son.

1. We may be inclined to make David the hero of this lesson. Why is it important that God be considered the hero of this lesson (and of all other biblical lessons)?

2. Against all odds, God enabled David to defeat the giant Goliath. Against all odds, God has defeated our greatest enemy—death—through His Son's death on the cross. How does God's defeat of our greatest enemy provide us comfort and encouragement when we face other enemies?

3. Explain the meaning of "the battle belongs to the Lord" for your life.

4. David chose to take drastic action against Goliath, using five smooth stones and a sling. How can we know when and how to take drastic actions in our lives? See Philippians 4:6 and James 1:5–6.

5. The account ended with victory: David defeated Goliath. Some of our "endings," however, may seem more like defeats. Do we then conclude that we failed to act according to God's will? Or what should we think? See Romans 8:31–39.

Catechism Connection

Examine the Catechism sections about Baptism in the opening for this session.

1. Read 1 Peter 3:20–21. Compare the blessings of water in the flood of Noah's day and the water of Baptism.

2. In the Large Catechism Martin Luther says that when our sins or conscience oppress us, we must retort, "I am baptized!" How can these words give us strength and comfort?

Send

To Do This Week

Family Connection

1. Review the events of this week's biblical account. Ask, "How is God the hero in each of these events?"

2. Describe how God has worked in your life through your Baptism, and how He continues to work in your life as you hear His Word.

3. Together draw a family mural depicting the phrase "the battle belongs to the Lord!" Consider how this phrase is evident in your family and in the lives of each of the members of your family.

Personal Reflection

1. Create a prayer using the sentence starter "Against all odds, God in Christ …"

2. Share with a friend or a loved one how God has demonstrated His kingship in your life.

3. Write the words "the battle belongs to the Lord" on a sheet of paper or a note card. Place the words in a conspicuous place where you will see them often.

For Next Week

In preparation for the next session skim Nehemiah 1:1–13:31. Then read Matthew 24:37–44; Luke 1:5–25; and Romans 13:11–14.

God Prepares the World for Jesus

(The Book of Nehemiah; Matthew 24:37–44;
Luke 1:5–25; Romans 13:11–14)

— Gather —

Theme: Stage Set

Key Point

God, who kept the promises He made long ago, continues to give His people the promised gifts of forgiveness of sins and eternal life.

Objectives

By the power of the Holy Spirit working through God's Word, we will
1. describe how God set perfectly the stage to fulfill His plan of salvation for the world;
2. confess our helpless and hopeless condition that would cause us without God's intervention in and through the person and work of Jesus to be hopelessly lost;
3. share with others God's plan of salvation for their lives.

Opening

Read the Second Petition of the Lord's Prayer and Martin Luther's explanation responsively:
All: Thy kingdom come.
Leader: What does this mean?
Group: The kingdom of God certainly comes by itself without our prayer, but we pray in this petition that it may come to us also.
Leader: How does God's kingdom come?
Group: God's kingdom comes when our heavenly Father gives us His Holy Spirit, so that by His grace we believe His holy

Word and lead godly lives here in time and there in eternity.

Introduction

We often hear or use the phrase the stage is set to describe our preparation for an event.

1. For what events in your life have you set the stage? How successful were you?

2. For what events in your life do you wish you had set the stage? Why?

3. In spite of all the stage-setting, we may still at times have difficulties. Why is this? Give an example.

God has perfectly set the stage for His plan of salvation. In today's lesson we witness God's activity in human events to prepare the world for His Son, our Savior. Jesus Christ.

Study

Reading the Text

David reigned from approximately 1010 to 970 B.C. Nehemiah began to govern the Jews in 445 B.C. During the intervening five centuries, the kingdom had been divided (1 Kings 11:29—33) and both halves destroyed (2 Kings 17:1—7; 2 Chronicles 36:11–21). Judah had been carried off to Babylon for 70 years, but, when Babylon herself was conquered by Persia in 537, the Jews had been allowed to return. A first contingent had returned and rebuilt the temple (536—516). More had come back in about 458 under the leadership of the priest Ezra. Yet by the time of Nehemiah, the walls of Jerusalem still lay in ruins. The story of Nehemiah, then, is the account of the rebuilding of the city in which Jesus Christ would complete His saving work. That, in turn, sets the stage for the announcement of the forerunner of Christ, John the Baptist.

Without its city-walls. Jerusalem was vulnerable. Moreover, the shambles made God's people a "reproach" and "disgrace" in the eyes of their neighbors (Nehemiah 2:17). Such a rubbish heap could never sere as the focal point of true worship (Psalm 122), as the inspiration to the chosen nation or the magnet to attract other nations (Psalm 48; 87), or as the site of God's eternal, saving act (Luke 13:33—35). The very salvation of the world was at stake.

Nehemiah, one of the many Jews who had not returned to Palestine, held a significant position in the Persian court. As "cup-bearer" to King Artaxerxes (Nehemiah 1:11), he was entrusted with protecting the king from assassination by poisoning. (Perhaps as a Jew he had reached such prominence due to the influence of former Queen Esther, who may still have been living at this time.)

When he heard of the plight of Jerusalem, Nehemiah did not go immediately to the king with his concern (1:1—2:8). Artaxerxes had already once ordered the rebuilding of Jerusalem stopped (Ezra 4:21—23), and Persian royal custom forbade approaching the king without invitation (Esther 4:11). For four months Nehemiah prayed, and when the opportune moment arrived, he offered another silent prayer before speaking (2:4).

Prayer is one of the striking elements of Nehemiah's story (4:4–5, 9; 5:19; 6:9, 14; 13:l4ff.). Frequently he interrupts his narration to address the Lord with a concern. Nehemiah was aware that his great task could be accomplished only by God's power, but he was equally confident that God would grant success (2:8, 20; 4:14–15, 20; 6:16; 7:5; 13:2). This was the encouragement that spurred the Jews to action. "I told them," Nehemiah said, "how the hand of my God had been favorable to me.... So they put their hands to the good work" (2:18, paraphrase).

Certainly they needed every measure of God's help. Local rivals conspired to frustrate the work (2:10, 19; 4:1–3, 7–8, 11; 6:1–13).

(The later intense hatred by the Jews for the Samaritans was largely based on these incidents.) Moreover, the task itself was monumental (3:1–32). The perimeter length of the wall was approximately one-and-a-half miles, although undoubtedly not all of it needed rebuilding. At least 10 gates had to be replaced. Some of the cliff on which the eastern wall had stood had apparently collapsed (2:14), so that a new foundation would have to be laid.

Remarkably, by God's hand and the teamwork of many hands, the wall was completed in 52 clays (6:15). The reproach had been turned to joyful celebration (12:27–43). The city could once again be a sanctuary for pure worship and hearing of God's Word (8:1–18; 13:1–31), a symbol of commitment to the Lord (9:1–10:39), and a place where justice was done (5:1–19).

Some 400 years later, it would also be the city where the long-anticipated events of God's salvation would begin to unfold (Luke 1:5–25). From his home in the hill country (1:39) Zechariah would go twice a year to Jerusalem to fulfill a week of priestly service. No doubt he was faithful in his duties, just as he and his wife, Elizabeth, were "blameless" before the Lord (1:6). They must have also been resigned to the will of God, for although they were elderly, they had no child.

As much as Zechariah and Elizabeth must have longed for a child, they shared with all the faithful of the day a greater longing. For over four centuries God had not spoken to His people by a prophet. Since coming home from Babylon, the Jews had been conquered frequently and now lived under Roman rule. God's silence and their humiliation created an unprecedented yearning for God to deliver on His promise of a Messiah, a Savior. The frenzy among some had even spawned a number of false messiahs (Acts 5:36—37). Might God's time be near?

This day Zechariah's time had finally come (L:8—9). Each day the priests on duty (perhaps as many as 50 men) would draw lots for responsibilities. The most sacred was to burn incense in the holy place (Exodus 30:6—8) at the conclusion of the service. (The incense symbolized that the prayers of the worshipers had been heard.) A priest was permitted this honor only once in his life, but with 24 orders of priests rotating, many would never receive the lot. Today the lot had fallen to Zechariah.

As Zechariah was completing his solemn rite, an angel suddenly appeared to the right of the altar (1:10–20). "Your prayers have been heard," the angel announced. Zechariah and Elizabeth would have a son, John, whose name means "the Lord is gracious." John would be a lifelong Nazirite like Samson and Samuel; he would be filled with the Holy Spirit from conception (see 1:41–44). Most important, he would fulfill the prophecy of a man like Elijah, bringing repentance and reconciliation (Malachi 4:5–6; Matthew 17:9–13).

The last element was indeed most important because the new Elijah would "make ready a people prepared for the Lord" (1:17). The prophet would prepare the way for the coining of the Messiah. God's time was now! If Zechariah's son was the forerunner, then the Christ, too, was near!

Would Zechariah's son be the forerunner? Zechariah wanted a sign to prove the angel's words. The request would have been appropriate if the messenger's identity were uncertain. But there was no question about the speaker: "I am Gabriel who stands in the presence of God." Zechariah's doubts had not been about the messenger, but about Cod's ability to perform the birth miracle. Zechariah would indeed have a sign from the Lord: he would be unable to speak until God fulfilled His word (Luke 1:20).

It was, however, only a temporary setback for Zechariah. Like so many others (1:14), he would soon be able to rejoice without limitation, because John's birth would herald the coming of the Messiah, the source of all joy.

Discussing the Text

1. Why was the rebuilding of the city walls of Jerusalem important? How does Nehemiah 4 illustrate this importance?

2. What is the significance of Nehemiah's frequent interruption of his narrative to address the Lord with his concerns?

3. Discuss the significance of Nehemiah's statement, "I told them the hand of my God had been favorable to me…. So they put their hands to the good work" (paraphrase of 2:18).

4. Why was it important for the Israelites to separate themselves from the foreigners (Nehemiah 9:2; 13:23–27)?

5. How was the hand of' the Lord evident in the account of Zechariah and Elizabeth?

6. Describe the sign given to Zechariah.

7. How would the birth of John herald the coming of the Messiah?

Apply

Taken together, these texts offer us a most helpful application: God's promises never fail. God had pledged to David a "house"—a family line—that would reign forever (2 Samuel 7:16), a "lamp" that would never go out (1 Kings 11:36). The house was established in Jesus. The lamp was lit in the saving work of David's Son, the Messiah. The destruction of Jerusalem had seemed to doom the promises, but God restored them with the city. Centuries of silence may have caused even the faithful to doubt whether God remembered Israel, but John's miraculous birth meant the Messiah would come to them. God's word will come true in His time.

So will all the promises of Christ, including the promise of His return at the end of time. He will be with us always (Matthew 28:20). He will, for the sake of His cross, receive us back in forgiveness every time we sin (1 John 1:8—9). He will take all who believe in Him to heaven someday (2 Timothy 4:8). He will freely give us all things (Romans 8:32).

1. How is the fact that God set the stage for salvation evident in this biblical account? in others?

2. Describe how God set the stage for your salvation.

3. How has God set the stage for you to share His plan of salvation with others? What guidelines does Jesus provide in Matthew 28:19–20 and Acts 1:8?

4. Reread the second paragraph of the "Apply" section of this session, replacing the future tense "will" with the present tense. Why is it important for us to focus on that which God has and continues to accomplish in our lives?

Catechism Connection

Review the Second Petition and Martin Luther's explanation in the Opening for this session.

1. What three aspects of the kingdom of God are revealed in Psalm 103:19; John 3:5; and 2 Timothy 4:18?

2. What roles does God give us in the kingdom of grace? See Acts 4:29 and 1 Peter 2:12.

3. Why need we not get discouraged with the work God gives us? See Isaiah 55:11.

Send

To Do This Week

Family Connection

1. Review each of the accounts during family devotions. Describe how each of the events "set the stage" for Jesus.

2. Review the events of the faith life of each member of your family. Include in the discussion major events in your life that God has used in order to draw you closer to Him (e.g., Baptism, Sunday school, confirmation, Holy Communion, worship).

3. Make a prayer list. Pray daily for the things you include on the list. Revise the list daily to include additional things your family wishes to pray for.

Personal Reflection

1. Spend time this week meditating on Romans 13:11–14. What is the significance of this passage for your life?

2. Consider how God works today in events to bring people closer to Him.

3. Pray that God would provide you new opportunities to share His plan of salvation with those who do not know Jesus.

For Next Week

Read Matthew 3:1–12 and Luke 1:57–80 in preparation for the next session.

Adult Leader Guide

Session 1

God Calls Moses

(Exodus 2–4)

Theme: "Why Me?"

Key Point and the Objectives

Ask volunteers to read aloud the objectives for this session.

Opening

Read the First Article and Martin Luther's explanation responsively. Then lead the group in prayer: Heavenly Father, when we feel overwhelmed by challenges that confront us, remind us of Your unlimited power and of Your great love for us—love so great that You sent Your only Son to rescue us from our sin. Forgive our sins and empower us to accept and carry out the tasks You place before us. We pray in Jesus' precious name. Amen.

Introduction

Discuss the questions. If your class is large you may wish to divide the class into small groups so that all have a chance to participate.

1. Answers will vary. We usually ask, "Why me?" when we encounter difficult situations or hardships in our lives.

2. Whenever we avoid or neglect opportunities to share God's love in Christ Jesus with others, we demonstrate a "why me?" attitude. Point out that whenever we sin we demonstrate a "why me?" attitude.

Ask a volunteer to read aloud the closing paragraph of this section.

Study

Reading the Text

Read aloud and invite volunteers to read aloud portions of the assigned Scripture. Then read aloud or skim the commentary. If time is short, you may wish to summarize the main points.

Discussing the Text

If your group is large you may want to divide into small groups to discuss the questions. This will provide everyone an opportunity to participate. Budget your time, so that you can reassemble the group to discuss the answers to the questions.

1. Moses' parents defied Pharaoh's order. They prepared a basket and hid Moses in it. They set the basket in the river. The baby was discovered and adopted by the daughter of Pharaoh. Moses grew up with the finest training, and yet his own mother was paid by Pharaoh's daughter to nurse him. God is able to overcome evil and to place people into situations where they will be able to accomplish His purposes.

2. Moses rashly attempted to rally his fellow Israelites against their oppressors by killing an Egyptian. He was forced to flee for his life. Not even foolish actions by one of God's servants can keep God from accomplishing His purposes.

3. Moses' objections included "I'm nobody," "The Egyptians don't know who You (God) are," "They won't buy my story," "I can't speak well," and "I am too scared." God's responses to Moses' objections included "I will be with you," "I AM WHO I AM," "This is so that they may believe that the Lord has appeared to you," "I will help you speak,"and "Your brother Aaron will speak to the people for you."

4. God continues to remain patient with Moses even as Moses objects to God's will. God responds promptly and lovingly to Moses' concerns.

Apply

Read aloud the opening paragraphs. Then discuss the questions that follow.

1. Often we respond as Moses did to God's call for us to serve. God continues to call, equip, and empower us to serve Him through His Word. When we disregard, ignore, or defy God's will for our lives, we act like Moses.

2. Answers will vary.

3. Answers will vary. Provide participants the opportunity to share their response with a partner or in a small group.

4. Answers will vary. As a minimum, all members of your group can encourage and support one another in their service to the Lord.

5. God's love for us in Christ Jesus motivates us to serve Him in our thoughts, words, and deeds.

Catechism Connection

1. Answers will vary.

2. We can't increase our faith with our own power. That's God's work. However, we *can* frequently participate in the means He uses to increase our faith: His Word and Holy Communion.

3. God will lead us to stop giving excuses and to accept the tasks He gives us, knowing He also will give us the power and resources we need to carry out those tasks.

Send

To Do This Week

Urge participants to complete the suggested activities before the next time you meet. Then close with prayer.

For Next Week

Urge participants to read Exodus 5:1–12:30 before the next time you meet.

Session 2

God Works to Deliver His People from Egypt

(Exodus 5:1–12:30)

Gather

Theme: Flexing His Muscle

Key Point and the Objectives

Invite volunteers to read aloud the key point and the objectives for this session.

Opening

Read responsively Psalm 33:12–22. Then lead the group in prayer: Lord, we know You really are worthy of our trust. Help us to put our hope in You today and every day. In Jesus' name we pray. Amen.

Introduction

Read aloud the opening paragraph. Then discuss the questions that follow. If your class is large, consider dividing it into small groups for the discussion sections of the session. This will provide everyone an opportunity to participate.

1. Answers will vary. Often when we believe we are being unjustly treated, we will flex our muscle.

2. Answers will vary.

Read aloud the closing paragraph.

Study

Reading the Text

Skim Exodus 5:1–12:30. Then read the commentary aloud, if time permits.

Discussing the Text

1. Do not spend too much time discussing each of the plagues. Point out that each plague was a miracle of God. The plagues demonstrate that God is in control of all things, including natural consequences, life, and death.

2. The plagues put God's power through Moses head to head with the Egyptian gods. The Nile (Hopi) was turned to blood, the frogs (goddess Heqt) became a nuisance, the bulls (Apis) died, and the sun (Amon–Ra) turned dark at God's command.

3. The change from grumbling to obedience demonstrates the power of God to change people's hearts. God uses whatever means He chooses, from the Egyptian oppression to God's power as demonstrated by the plagues to the power of His Word spoken through Moses and Aaron.

4. Jesus, the sinless Lamb of God, was slaughtered on a wooden cross to provide life to those who believe in Him. The angel of death has no power over us. The blood of Christ covers our sin. We will live forever with Jesus in heaven, not because of what we have done, but because of what He has done for us.

Apply

Read aloud the opening paragraphs. Then discuss the questions that follow.

1. The spiritual outcome for those who live in ignorance of God or who openly defy Him is the same—eternal death.

2. The children of Israel did nothing to deserve the deliverance that God provided to them. We have done nothing to deserve the deliverance from sin, death, and the power of the devil that God won for us through His Son's death on the cross.

3. When we celebrate the Lord's Supper, the church family remembers the suffering and death of Jesus, the Lamb, and the deliverance He won for us over sin and death. In the Lord's Sup-

per we receive the true body and true blood of Jesus in, with, and under the bread and wine. When we eat His body and drink His blood, we receive the forgiveness of sins and proclaim to the world that Jesus Christ is Lord. The Hebrews celebrated the Passover as the ultimate reminder of God's victory and deliverance of His people. The family celebrated with a sacrificed lamb, unleavened bread, wine, and other elements to remind them how God rescued them from slavery.

4. For example, a shadow provides an outline of a person's appearance, but we may be surprised when we see the details in person. In a similar way the Old Testament festivals showed an outline of God's saving action, but the people were surprised by the details of the reality. It would be foolish to focus on the shadow instead of the reality.

5. Answers will vary. Whenever we seek opportunities to serve God, we praise and give glory to God for that which He first gave us—forgiveness of sins and eternal life through Jesus' death on the cross.

6. Answers will vary. Remind participants that the Lord continues to work mightily today through His Word and His Sacraments to create and to strengthen saving faith in Jesus.

Catechism Connection

1. Only by the power of the Holy Spirit can we believe that God still loves us when He allows tragedy to strike us. He empowers us to place everything into the context of the salvation Jesus earned for us (Romans 8:31–39) and to yearn for that ultimate victory.

2. When we turn to God's Word we learn that even though the wicked may prosper here on earth, they face a final destiny of ruin and destruction. Believers, on the other hand, know God is our refuge here on earth and that He will take us to live with Him in glory eternally.

Send

To Do This Week

Urge participants to complete one or more of the suggested activities before the next time you meet. Then close with prayer.

For Next Week

Urge participants to read Exodus 12:31–42 and 13:17–15:21 in preparation for the next meeting.

Session 3

God Leads His People Out of Egypt

(Exodus 12:31–42; 13:17–15:21)

Gather

Theme: Follow the Leader

Key Point and the Objectives

Read aloud or ask volunteers to read aloud the key point and the objectives.

Opening

Read the Second Commandment and Martin Luther's explanation responsively. Then lead the group in prayer: Heavenly Father, as You led the people of Israel out of the bondage of slavery in Egypt, so You have provided us a way out of the slavery of sin, death, and the devil through Your Son Jesus. Strengthen our faith, we pray, and empower us to walk in Your paths every day of our lives. Hear us for Jesus' sake. Amen.

Introduction

Read aloud the opening paragraphs. Then discuss the questions that follow. If your class is large, consider putting participants into small groups for the discussion sections of the lesson. This will give everyone a chance to participate.

1. Answers will vary. Each of the "leaders" listed in the Study Guide—if they become number one in a person's life—can have grave consequences. They may promise happiness, peace, or joy, but they can lead to troubles and hardships. Ultimately, the wages of sin is death.

2. Other leaders might include people, food, and the pursuit of

happiness. Answers will vary.

3. Our sinful nature causes us to choose things and people other than God as our leader. God in His love for us knew that on our own we would never choose Him. For this reason God sent His only Son, Jesus, into the world to live a perfect life on our behalf and then suffer the consequences for our sin—death. Through Jesus' death on the cross God has "re-purchased" us—redeemed us—from our old sinful self. God's love for us empowers us to keep Him number one in our lives.

Read aloud the closing paragraph.

Study

Reading the Text

Invite volunteers to read aloud portions of the Scripture lesson. Then read aloud the commentary or, if time is short, summarize the important points.

Discussing the Text

1. God planned and orchestrated the events leading up to and including the Exodus. These included the first nine plagues, the final plague, moving two million people quickly out of Egypt, providing for the physical needs of all of His people, leading the people by a cloud of smoke during the day and a pillar of fire at night, and parting the Red Sea so that the Israelites could cross on dry ground.

2. These events show that the God of Israel was the one true God who was always in control.

3. Remembering how God used His power to save the nation gave the people courage during their wilderness journeys and at other times when they faced seemingly impossible challenges, such as before, during, and after the Babylonian captivity.

4. The people responded to God's protection, deliverance, and guidance by singing praises and thanks to Him.

Apply

Read aloud the opening paragraphs. Then discuss the questions that follow.

1. Answers will vary. Ultimately, God demonstrated His leadership in our lives when He sent His only Son into this world to suffer and to die on a cross for our sins.

2. The Israelites saw the destructive force of water, but passed through into a new life. In Holy Baptism the sinner is drowned and dies, but is raised again to a new life in Christ Jesus (Romans 6:4). Through Holy Baptism God makes us His children. He frees us from sin and death through Holy Baptism.

3. Answers will vary. Recounting God's gracious work in our lives provides us an opportunity to praise and thank Him. The liturgy, hymns, and living service allow us to respond to God's gracious act of salvation.

Catechism Connection

1. Special opportunities to honor God's name arise when we observe any blessing God has given to us or someone we know—blessings such as forgiveness of sins, healing of a disease, provision of a necessity of life, or protection from harm. We can honor God's name in public worship, family devotions, in daily conversation, and the like.

2. The references from Psalms invite us to use God's name in prayer, in praise, and in thanksgiving.

Send

To Do This Week

Urge participants to complete one or more of the suggested activities prior to the next time the class meets. Then close with prayer.

For Next Week

Urge participants to read Exodus 16–17 in preparation for the next class meeting.

Session 4

God Gives His People Food and Water

(Exodus 16–17)

Gather

Theme: Like a Broken Record

Key Point and the Objectives

Invite volunteers to read aloud the key point and the objectives.

Opening

In unison read aloud Isaiah 58:9–11. Then lead the group in prayer: Heavenly Father, we know that You provide all that we need for our lives, but at times we still grumble and complain. Forgive us, we pray, and fill our hearts with thankfulness and trust. We pray in Jesus' name. Amen.

Introduction

Say, "You sound like a broken record." Ask, "What does this mean?" Then ask a participant to read aloud the paragraph explaining the saying. Discuss the questions that follow. If your class is large you may wish to create small groups for the discussion portions of the session so that everyone has an opportunity to participate.

1. Answers will vary. Many times parents may sound like broken records to their children, particularly if a child has to be asked or reminded to do something over and over again.

2. We sin over and over and over. On our own we are helpless to avoid or to conquer our propensity to sin. Only God's love for us in Christ Jesus can break the cycle of sin.

Read aloud the closing paragraph of this section.

Study

Reading the Text

Read aloud or invite volunteers to read aloud portions of Exodus 16:1–17:16. Then read the commentary section. If time is short, you may wish to summarize the important information included in the commentary.

Discussing the Text

1. God provided quail and manna for food. He provided water from the "rock at Horeb."

2. God provided for all of the needs of His people. They had done nothing to deserve God's gracious provisions. He continued to provide for His people even when they complained. The people at first were thankful for that which God provided. Their thankfulness quickly turned to grumbling. They complained about everything.

3. By providing manna only six days a week, God taught His people to trust Him.

4. God wanted the people to know that they could trust in and live by God's Word. During the centuries that followed, God gave frequent reminders of the truth, using spokespersons such as Solomon and Ezra.

Apply

Read aloud the opening paragraphs. Then discuss the questions that follow.

1. We at times complain about that which we don't have, rather than focusing on all that God has provided us.

2. Answers may include taking time to listen, words of encouragement, actions to help one another, and the like.

3. God continues to offer His love and forgiveness through Jesus Christ to sinners. Like a broken record, God continues to forgive repentant sinners.

4. God has provided for our greatest need—life. By God's grace, through faith in Christ Jesus, God provides forgiveness of sins and eternal life. Only Jesus can deliver us from eternal death.

5. Answers will vary. Urge participants to share specific ways in which they can demonstrate thankfulness to God for all that He has provided to them.

Catechism Connection

1. God forbids cursing and swearing falsely.

2. Answers will vary. Those who curse or who swear falsely may want to cover up their insecurity or fit in with the crowd.

3. Avoid the cursing and swearing; answer with a simple *yes* or *no*. When an oath is appropriate (as in court or a marriage vow), do not break the oath.

Send

To Do This Week

Urge participants to complete one or more of the suggested activities prior to the next time the class meets. Then close with prayer.

For Next Week

Urge participants to prepare for the next class session by reading Exodus 19:1–20:21; 24; 32; and 35:4–29.

Session 5

God Helps Us Follow Him

(Exodus 19:1–20:21; 24; 32; 35:4–29)

Gather

Theme: Spelled Out

Key Point and the Objectives

Invite volunteers to read aloud the key point and the objectives for this session.

Opening

Read responsively the selected verses from Psalm 51. Then lead the group in prayer: Thank You, Father, for sending Your Son to suffer the punishment we deserve because of our sin. We pray, send the Holy Spirit to motivate and empower us to follow You always, for Jesus' sake. Amen.

Introduction

1. Answers will vary. Most of us have clearly spelled out our expectations to someone only to have him/her disregard or defy them.

2. Whenever we break a commandment we disregard or defy God's will. We are born with original sin, and, apart from God's forgiveness and grace, we cannot fulfill His expectations.

Read aloud the closing paragraph of this section.

Study

Reading the Text

Read aloud or invite volunteers to read aloud the portions of Scripture. If time is short, you may wish to summarize the events that occur in each of the portions. Then read aloud or summarize the important facts discussed in the commentary.

Discussing the Text

1. Write down each of the Ten Commandments. Point out that each commandment tells us either what to do or what not to do. For example, the First Commandment, "You shall have no other gods before Me," tells us we should not worship other gods, and that we should only worship the true God. The Fourth Commandment, "Honor your father and your mother," tells us to honor our parents and not to dishonor them.

2. The first use of the Law is a "curb to sin." God means business. His Law was to serve as a deterrent to sin. The second use of the Law is a "mirror to sin." The Law shows people their sin and their desperate need for a Savior. The third use of the Law is sometimes described as a "rule." Christians are motivated in response to God's love for them in Christ Jesus to do that which God commands.

3. God wants His people to see their need for an intercessor for their sins. On their own they are helpless to restore their broken relationship to God. Moses is a precursor to the once-and-for-all Mediator—Jesus Christ—who received the punishment we deserved because of our sin, to buy us back from the clutches of sin and death.

4. Through Moses God gave laws and rituals that were shadows of what was to come through Jesus. The Old Testament sacrifices had to be repeated regularly, while Jesus gave a once-for-all sacrifice for our sins.

Apply

Read aloud the opening paragraphs. Then discuss the questions that follow.

1. Answers will vary. God's covenant with us is one-sided. God declares, "You are my people through faith in Christ Jesus." We have done nothing to earn or to keep the covenant God established with us. Instead, God's covenant with us was initiated by Him and continues to be sustained by Him.

2. God's love in Christ Jesus motivates us to do that which God desires.

3. We are free from sin, death, and the power of the devil. But we are not free to do whatever we wish. God desires that we live according to His will.

Catechism Connection

1. The people brought so many gifts for the tabernacle that Moses finally had to say, "Enough!"

2. The psalmist offered to the Lord the expressions of goodness He desired.

3. Paul encourages us to share our gifts with others.

Send

To Do This Week

Urge participants to complete one or more of the suggested activities before the class meets again. Then close with prayer.

For Next Week

Ask participants to read Numbers 21:4–9 and Joshua 3–4 in preparation for the next class meeting.

Session 6

God Saves His People

(Numbers 21:4–9; Joshua 3–4)

Gather

Theme: Lifted Up—Uplifted

Key Point and the Objectives

Invite volunteers to read aloud the key point and the objectives.

Opening

Read the First Commandment and Martin Luther's explanation responsively. Then lead the group in prayer: Thank You, Father, for the saving work You accomplished through Jesus. Send us Your Holy Spirit, we pray, and move us to share this Good News with our families, friends, and co-workers. In Jesus' name. Amen.

Introduction

Invite volunteers to read aloud each of the sentences. Then discuss the questions that follow. If your class is large, divide it into small groups for the discussion sections of the session so that everyone has an opportunity to participate.

1. Answers will vary.

2. Only Jesus lifted on a cross is able to give us a lift, lift our spirits, and uplift us by His Word.

Read aloud the closing paragraph of this section.

Study

Reading the Text

Invite volunteers to read aloud portions of Numbers 21:4–9 and Joshua 3–4. Then read aloud or summarize the commentary.

Discussing the Text

1. The spies reported to the Israelites that the people of Canaan would be impossible to defeat. The people of Israel rebelled against their leaders, Joshua and Caleb, and against God. God decreed that this generation of Israelites would never enter the Promised Land. Instead they would wander in the wilderness for 40 years until all the people over the age of 20 died.

2. The people rebelled against God and Moses. God responded to the people's rebellion by sending "fiery serpents" into the camp. As soon as the people repented, God instructed Moses to make a serpent of bronze and raise it up on a pole. Anyone who looked to the bronze serpent survived the snakebite.

3. Jesus was lifted up on a pole, the cross. All who look to the cross in faith survive their sin-sickness and live.

4. The ark of the covenant represents God's presence with His people.

5. The God who delivered them from Egypt continued to protect them, guide them, and deliver them.

Apply

Read aloud the opening paragraphs. Then discuss the questions that follow.

1. God used the serpent on the pole as a means to save His people.

2. God blesses us as we look to the cross of Christ. Specifically, God provides by His grace, through faith, forgiveness of sins and eternal life.

3. God continues to use means today to bestow His blessings on people. The means of grace are the Word and the Sacraments. Through His Word God provides His faith-creating and faith-sustaining power. By the power of the Holy Spirit working through

water and the Word, God claims us as His own dear children through Holy Baptism. In the Lord's Supper God provides the body and blood of Jesus for the forgiveness of sins. The simple substances of water, bread, and wine receive their power from God's Word.

4. The people were to tell their children about God's saving action. Similar opportunities exist today when we tell our children what takes place in Baptism or the Lord's Supper—or when we see a rainbow, receive needed rain, and so forth.

Catechism Connection

1. Idolaters have no inheritance in heaven. Instead, an eternity in hell awaits them unless, through faith, they turn to Jesus, who died to pay for their sins.

2. Answers will vary.

3. Satan is powerful. Therefore we must receive God's power in order to conquer idolatry.

Send

To Do This Week

Urge participants to complete one or more of the suggested activities before the class meets again. Then close with prayer.

For Next Week

Urge participants to read Joshua 3–4 and 5:13–6:27 in preparation for the next meeting.

Session 7

God Gives Victory at Jericho

(Joshua 3–4; 5:13–6:27)

Gather

Theme: A Battle Won!

Key Point and the Objectives

Invite volunteers to read aloud the key point and the objectives for this session.

Opening

Read responsively the words of Psalm 129:1–4. Then lead the group in prayer: Thank You, heavenly Father, for preserving us during the difficult times of our lives. We pray that You will continue to display Your power and mercy in our lives, and that You will finally take us to live with You in heaven. Hear us for Jesus' sake. Amen.

Introduction

Read the opening statement. Then discuss the questions that follow. If your class is large, consider dividing it into small groups for the discussion portions of this session. This will give everyone an opportunity to participate.

1. Answers will vary.

2. Answers will vary. We need to be careful when choosing battles to fight. Some are just not worth the effort.

3. We are unable to choose the spiritual battle that goes on at all times—the battle that is waged between our sinful self and our new self in Christ.

Read aloud the closing paragraph of this section.

Study

Reading the Text

Invite volunteers to read aloud portions of Joshua 3:1–4:24 and 5:13–6:27. Then summarize the important information included in the commentary.

Discussing the Text

1. God developed and delivered the battle plan. God is in complete control. Only God could conquer the city of Jericho. Only God could conquer the city in the way He planned.

2. Seven priests with seven trumpets were to lead the people, who would march around the city once each day for seven days. On the seventh day, the priests and the people were to march around the city seven times, blow the trumpets, and shout. God would take care of the rest.

3. Answers will vary. Most military experts would probably describe the battle plan as bizarre or impossible.

4. Joshua followed the orders precisely because he understood that it would be God fighting the battle.

5. God ordered the soldiers to kill everyone, lest the people of Jericho lead Israel into worshiping their gods.

6. Rahab, a prostitute, who earlier had harbored two Israelite spies, was spared. Rahab would become an ancestor to Jesus.

7. In addition to any military advantage, surely this victory increased the peoples' confidence that God really was on their side, that He would grant success to the conquest of Canaan.

8. They would suffer abuse from the Canaanite people and finally would perish.

Apply

Read aloud the opening paragraphs. Then discuss the questions that follow.

1. Answers will vary. Don't force anyone to share.

2. Again, answers will vary.

3. God is in complete control. He is able to accomplish anything He desires. God desires good for His people.

4. We have nothing to fear, not even death. For through His death, Jesus conquered death; and through His resurrection, Jesus proclaimed victory for us over sin, death, and the power of the devil.

5. Give participants time to write a short prayer of thanksgiving and praise to God for winning the battle over sin, death, and the power of the devil. Use the prayers during the closing worship activity.

Catechism Connection

1. The cited passages affirm that the only true God is the triune God: Father, Son, and Holy Spirit, three distinct persons in one divine being.

2. God demands reverence toward Him. Discuss ways to show this reverence.

3. God requires that we love Him with all our heart, soul, and mind. Thus, only through faith in Jesus can we be saved.

Send

To Do This Week

Urge participants to complete one or more of the suggested activities before the class meets again. Then close with prayer.

For Next Week

Urge participants to read Judges 6–7 and 13–16 before the next class meeting.

Session 8

God Provides Victory through Judges

(Judges 6–7; 13–16)

Gather

Theme: History Repeats Itself

Key Point and the Objectives

Invite volunteers to read aloud the key point and the objectives for this session.

Opening

Read the Fifth Petition and Luther's explanation responsively. Then lead the group in prayer: Thank You, heavenly Father, for forgiving our sins instead of giving us the punishment we deserve. Empower us, we pray, to forgive those who sin against us. May our lives demonstrate our love for You. In Jesus' name we pray. Amen.

Introduction

1. Answers will vary. People rarely learn from their mistakes. The history of humanity demonstrates that people are unable to get along without repeating the same mistakes made by earlier generations. Although we witness destruction and pointlessness of war, wars continue.

2. God continues to forgive us in spite of our sin. We sin. We recognize our sin and repent. God forgives us through faith in Christ Jesus.

Read aloud the closing paragraph.

Study

Reading the Text

Read aloud or skim the portion of Scripture. Then read aloud or summarize the commentary.

Discussing the Text

1. In complacency toward the Canaanites, the Israelites allowed heathens to live among them. As God predicted, Israel began to follow the lead of the pagan Canaanites and worship their gods.

2. Israel would fall into idolatry, God would allow an enemy to torment Israel, Israel would repent and cry out to the Lord, God would send a deliverer to defeat the invader and judge the people for a time.

3. God gave Israel over to the Midianites and Amalekites. The Israelites repented of their sin. God sent Gideon to deliver the people.

4. The Philistines became a new adversary for the Israelites. Israel deserted the Lord and was powerless against the Philistines. God remained faithful to His people. God sent Samson to defeat the Philistines.

5. God continued to remain faithful to His people. Although powerless to help themselves, God provided judges to deliver His people from oppression.

6. God preserved the nation, keeping the promise He made to Abraham.

Apply

Read aloud or invite volunteers to read aloud the opening paragraphs. Then discuss the questions that follow.

1. People continue to sin. People continue to repent of their sin. God in Christ delivers people from their sin through His Son's death on the cross. This cycle was not only present during the time of the judges, but has been present throughout history and continues to be present today.

2. God never tires of offering His love and forgiveness through faith in Christ Jesus to repentant sinners.

3. Only the love of God in Christ Jesus enables, empowers, and motivates us to follow God's commands.

4. The woman washed Jesus' feet with her tears and hair. Our responses may vary.

5. Provide participants time to write a brief prayer thanking God for His continual love and forgiveness through Jesus. Use the completed prayers during the closing activity.

Catechism Connection

1. We confess that we sin every day and deserve nothing but punishment for those sins.

2. It shows that we truly believe that God has forgiven us.

Send

To Do This Week

Urge participants to complete one or more of the suggested activities before the class meets again. Then close with prayer.

For Next Week

Urge participants to read the Book of Ruth in preparation for the next study time.

Session 9

God Blesses Ruth

(The Book of Ruth)

Gather

Theme: Devoted

Key Point and the Objectives

Invite volunteers to read aloud the key point and the objectives for this session.

Opening

Read the Fourth Commandment and Luther's explanation responsively. Then lead the group in prayer: When troubles threaten to overwhelm us, dear God, help us remember Your love and faithfulness. Strengthen us with Your mighty power, and move us to act in ways that demonstrate our love for You. In Jesus' name we pray. Amen.

Introduction

Discuss the questions. If your class is large, you may wish to divide it into small groups for the discussion portions of the session so that everyone has an opportunity to participate.

1. Answers will vary.

2. We demonstrate devotion in many ways—being there when someone needs us, listening to someone, sharing joys, crying together as sorrows are shared, and so on.

3. Answers will vary. Be sensitive to participants who may feel that no one is devoted to them.

Read aloud or invite a volunteer to read aloud the closing paragraph of this section.

Study

Reading the Text

Summarize the Book of Ruth and the commentary section.

Discussing the Text

1. Naomi lost her husband and two sons.

2. Ruth's decision to go with Naomi was an expression of faith in the God of Israel. This motivated her tender loyalty to Naomi, her mother-in-law.

3. Boaz was God-fearing and wealthy. He was also a close relative of Naomi's late husband.

4. The kinsman-redeemer had the duty of redeeming the widow by making her his own wife and maintaining the family line of the deceased kinsman.

5. The other relative was not eager to marry the widow and raise up an heir for the deceased.

6. Participants may mention Ruth's dedication to Naomi, the actions of Boaz, a Moabite becoming an ancestor of Jesus, and the like. Answers will vary.

Apply

Read aloud or invite volunteers to read aloud the opening paragraphs. Then discuss the questions that follow.

1. Jesus came to redeem all people—Jews and Gentiles—from sin, death, and the power of the devil.

2. Ruth is a believer in the one true God and trusts that God will be with her even in loneliness and poverty. She believes that life with Him will be more blessed than anything she might have without Him. Ruth's loyalty to her mother-in-law and the God of her husband's family also reveals trust in God's grace, and a loving responsibility to care for family as God first cared for her.

3. Boaz purchased Naomi back—redeemed her—from a life doomed to despair. In a sense Boaz provided a new life for Naomi. Jesus redeemed us from our sin. He gave us a new life in Him.

4. God's love in Christ motivates us to love as He first loved us. We demonstrate devotion to others in many ways—by listening, by helping, and by encouraging, to name just a few. Answers will vary.

Catechism Connection

1. Ruth loved and cherished Naomi, her mother-in-law.

2. Answers will vary. Care for parents and grandparents may include making daily phone calls, providing for their needs in their homes, bringing them into your homes, arranging nursing-home care, and so forth.

3. We must disobey authorities when they order us to do something contrary to God's commandments.

Send

To Do This Week

Urge participants to complete one or more of the suggested activities before the next class session. Then close with prayer.

For Next Week

Urge participants to read 1 Samuel 1:1–2:11 and 3:1–21 in preparation for their study in Session 10.

Session 10

God Calls Samuel

(1 Samuel 1:1–2:11; 3:1–21)

Gather

Theme: Overlooked, Unimportant, and Insecure

Key Point and the Objectives

Invite volunteers to read aloud the key point and the objectives.

Opening

Read the Introduction to the Lord's Prayer and Luther's explanation responsively. Then pray the entire Lord's Prayer together.

Introduction

Discuss the questions. If your class is large, consider dividing it into small groups so that everyone has an opportunity to participate.

1. Answers will vary.

2. What a marvelous statement! Jesus came to earth to suffer and to die for me—so that I might have forgiveness of sins and eternal life.

Read aloud the closing paragraph.

Study

Reading the Text

Read aloud or invite volunteers to read aloud portions of 1 Samuel 3:1–21 and 8:1–11:15. Summarize the important information included in the commentary.

Discussing the Text

1. Hannah was childless. In Israelite society a barren woman was stigmatized as rejected by God.

2. Hannah promised that if the Lord would give her a son, she would dedicate the child to serve Him as a Nazirite.

3. The song of Hannah is often called the "Magnificat of the Old Testament" because it parallels the song of Mary before the birth of Jesus. Both women sing God's inspired words that declare God to be strong, victorious, generous, and the champion of the humble servant of the Lord. Both songs anticipate God's work through His anointed, the Savior Jesus.

4. God spoke to Samuel during a time when visions or words of the Lord were rare.

5. God tells Samuel the bad news about Eli. God will punish the sons of Eli for their sinful indulgences.

6. Only God knows that which is in the hearts of people. God chooses those who seem most insignificant or unimportant to serve Him and His people. God equips these people for service. God does not select those whom the world would select. Instead, He chooses the most unlikely, that through them His grace might be revealed.

Apply

Read aloud or invite volunteers to read aloud the opening paragraphs of this section. Then discuss the questions that follow.

1. Throughout history and even today, God uses the most insignificant people to accomplish His will and purpose. Consider David, a shepherd boy. Consider Mary, a poor young woman.

2. Answers will vary. God makes me worthy through faith in Christ Jesus—worthy to serve Him.

3. Answers will vary. Invite participants to explore new ways God might possibly use them.

4. Only Jesus can give us worth and esteem that will last forever. Our search for *self*-worth and *self*-esteem are meaningless without the *Christ* worth and *Christ* esteem offered as a gift of God through faith in Jesus.

5. Share with those who feel overlooked, unimportant, or inse-

cure of the worth that God has provided to them through Christ Jesus.

Catechism Connection

1. Through faith we have become children of God; He truly is our Father.

2. The Father loves us dearly.

3. Even when we feel we can't pray, God assures us that the Spirit prays for us and that God is working for our good.

Send

To Do This Week

Urge participants to complete one or more of the suggested activities before the next class session. Then close with prayer.

For Next Week

Urge participants to read 1 Samuel 3 and 8–11 before the next meeting.

Session 11

God Gives Leaders to Israel

(1 Samuel 3; 8–11)

Gather

Theme: Like All the Others

Key Point and the Objectives

Invite volunteers to read aloud the key points of the objectives.

Opening

Read the Catechism sections responsively. Then lead the group in prayer: We confess, dear Father, that we are worthy of none of the rich blessings You shower upon us. We pray, lead us to receive Your gifts with thanksgiving and to use those gifts in service to You. In Jesus' name we pray. Amen.

Introduction

Read aloud or invite a volunteer to read aloud the opening paragraph. Then discuss the questions that follow. If your class is large, you may want to divide it into small groups so that everyone has an opportunity to participate.

1. We must admit that at times we cave in to peer pressure. Answers will vary.

2. As we try to be like others, we may lose sight of that which is most important—God. Whenever anyone or anything other than God becomes number one in our lives, we break the First Commandment.

Read aloud the closing paragraph.

Study

Reading the Text

Survey 1 Samuel 3:1–21 and 8:1–11:15. Then read aloud or summarize the important facts included in the commentary.

Discussing the Text

1. The elders' request troubled Samuel. The desire for the king was not the issue. Instead, the reason for wanting a king was the problem. God's people wanted to be "like all the other nations." They believed their neighbors' kings provided greater protection from enemies than they had experienced in the past. The irony of Israel's request was that they wanted to be like the very kingdoms that the Lord, their real King, had subdued in the past.

2. God gave the people a king. God, in His love for His people, provided a "man after His own heart," who by contrast to other nations' kings would be a modest servant and a follower of God's Word and ways.

3. The Spirit of the Lord came upon Saul and changed his heart.

4. Samuel gave Saul encouragement from the Lord. He honored Saul at a banquet. He spent hours in private instruction with Saul. He anointed Saul. He gave Saul three convincing signs that God would be with him.

5. God brought swift victory. Samuel summoned the people of Israel to Gilgal, Israel's first place of worship in Canaan, to "reaffirm the kingship" (of God Himself). Only then did the ceremonies confirm Saul as the king.

Apply

Read aloud or invite a volunteer to read aloud the opening paragraphs. Then discuss the questions that follow.

1. Anytime we sin, we are rejecting what God desires of us. Anything that, or anyone who, becomes number one in our lives other than God is an idol. We break the First Commandment whenever we replace God as number one in our lives with someone or something else.

2. God continues to invite us through His Word to receive the forgiveness of sins Jesus won for us on the cross. Yet God loves us like He loved His people of the Old Testament. He loves us like the Father loved the prodigal son. He speaks of His love for us in the Word and Sacraments. His ongoing love can give us comfort, hope, joy, and peace.

3. God is in control of our lives. Anytime we place our trust in someone or something other than God, we separate ourselves from Him. God continues to call us to Him through the Gospel, offering only that which He can give—forgiveness of sins and eternal life through faith in Christ Jesus.

4. Through the Gospel we receive the Spirit of God, who transforms us to become more like God, men and women after His own heart.

Catechism Connection

1. An infant receives the Spirit of God when he or she is baptized.

2. When Jesus says to baptize "all nations," this includes infants. Jesus also tells adults to "receive the kingdom of God like a little child."

3. By our own merits we can never become or remain members of God's kingdom. We continue to need the Spirit, who comes to us in Baptism and remains with us throughout our lives—or until we reject Him.

Send

To Do This Week

Urge participants to complete one or more of the suggested activities before the class meets again. Then close with prayer.

For Next Week

Urge participants to read 1 Samuel 13:1–15 and 15:1–17:54 in preparation for the next session.

Session 12

God Chooses David

(1 Samuel 13:1–15; 15:1–17:54)

Gather

Theme: Against All Odds

Key Point and the Objectives

Read aloud or invite volunteers to read aloud the key point and the objectives.

Opening

Read the Catechism sections responsively. Then lead the group in prayer: Though troubles may seem to overwhelm us at times, heavenly Father, we know You are able to provide the help and strength we need. We pray, keep us in Your gracious care and lead us to trust You in all circumstances. In Jesus' name we pray. Amen.

Introduction

Discuss the questions. If your class is large, consider dividing it into small groups so that everyone has an opportunity to participate in the discussion portions of the session.

1. Answers will vary.

2. Each of the endings focused on what people were able to accomplish against what seemed to be impossible odds.

3. Answers will vary. God in Christ saved us from sin, provides for us eternal life, forgives our sin, loves us always, enables us to love others, and so on.

Read aloud or invite a volunteer to read aloud the closing paragraph.

Study

Reading the Text

Skim 1 Samuel 13:1–15 and 15:1–17:54. Then summarize the main points discussed in the commentary.

Discussing the Text

1. Israel's human king was to prefigure the great King of the Jews, Jesus.

2. Saul panicked and offered the sacrifice to God that Samuel was to offer. Saul overruled God's command by sparing the king of the Amalekites and the best of their flocks. Worse yet, when Samuel confronted Saul, he lied.

3. Saul went his own way and exalted himself, rather than listening to and obeying God's Word.

4. David, the shepherd boy, prefigured Jesus, the Good Shepherd, who would lay down His life for His sheep.

5. Against all odds, David was able to defeat Goliath. David knew that the victory belonged to the Lord. God enabled David to defeat Goliath and win the battle against the Philistines.

Apply

Read aloud or invite volunteers to read aloud the opening paragraphs. Then discuss the questions that follow.

1. God is always the hero of Scripture. The biblical characters simply show the power of God to work through the simplest of people.

2. We have nothing to fear. God has defeated our greatest enemy—death—through the death of His only Son, Jesus. We need not fear death, for Jesus has won eternal life for us.

3. All battles, including the greatest battle of all—the battle against sin, death, and the power of the devil—God has won for me.

4. We pray that God would lead us to know what to do. Then, trusting His guidance, we act.

5. We may never know whether we "did the right thing" because we do not always know the outcome God desires. We do know, however, that nothing can separate us from God's love.

Catechism Connection

1. The waters of the great flood saved Noah and his family from the evil that surrounded them. The water of Baptism saves us by giving us the blessings of Jesus' victory over sin, death, and the devil.

2. Luther continues, "And if I am baptized, I have the promise that I shall be saved and have eternal life." Thus, remembering our Baptism gives strength and comfort for our daily lives.

Send

To Do This Week

Urge participants to complete one or more of the suggested activities before the next class session. Then close with prayer.

For Next Week

Urge participants to skim Nehemiah 1:1–13:31 and to read Matthew 24:37–44; Luke 1:5–25; and Romans 13:11–14 in preparation for the coming session.

Session 13
God Prepares the World for Jesus

(The Book of Nehemiah; Matthew 24:37–44;
Luke 1:5–25; Romans 13:11–14)

Gather

Theme: Stage Set

Key Point and the Objectives

Read aloud or invite a volunteer to read aloud the Law/Gospel focus.

Objectives

Invite volunteers to read aloud the key point and the objectives for this session.

Opening

Read the Second Petition and Luther's explanation responsively. Then lead the group in prayer: Heavenly Father, once You used Nehemiah, Zechariah, and others to prepare the world for the coming of the Savior. Open our hearts, we pray, to accept the roles You have given us to be Your instruments today. Hear us for Jesus' sake. Amen.

Introduction

Read aloud the opening sentence. Then discuss the questions that follow. If your class is large, you may wish to divide it into small groups so that everyone has the opportunity to participate during the discussion sections of the session.

1. Answers will vary. Often people set the stage for their career by preparing themselves in college. We might set the stage for our successful marriage by selecting the person with whom we would like to spend the rest of our lives.

2. Answers will vary.

3. We cannot anticipate all that might occur. All the stage-setting in the world does not take into account that we are sinful human beings who live in a sinful world. Sin affects our lives and the plans we make.

Study

Reading the Text

Read aloud the assigned portions of Scripture. If time is short, summarize the portions of Scripture using the commentary in the Study Guide.

Discussing the Text

1. The building of the city walls was imperative, because with-out it the city was vulnerable to attack. Enemies tried to stop the rebuilding.

2. Nehemiah frequently interrupts his narrative to address the Lord with a concern. Nehemiah relies upon the Lord for all.

3. Answers will vary. Motivated by God's love for him (the hand of God), Nehemiah serves the Lord.

4. Intermarriage could easily lead to worship of other gods and lead to a nation that no longer waited for the promised Messiah.

5. God selected Zechariah and Elizabeth to advance His plan for salvation. The Lord would provide a childless, elderly couple a son.

6. Zechariah was unable to speak until God fulfilled His Word.

7. As God had promised, John was born to prepare the way for the Savior, the Messiah who was to come.

Apply

Read aloud or invite volunteers to read aloud the opening paragraphs. Then discuss the questions that follow.

1. God set the stage for salvation of all people immediately following the fall into sin by Adam and Eve. Every action God takes throughout the Old Testament is in preparation for His plan of salvation that would be fulfilled in the person and through the work of His only Son, Jesus Christ.

2. Answers will vary. Invite volunteers to share their faith-story. Urge volunteers to focus on what God has done for them.

3. Through His Word and Sacrament the Holy Spirit works to strengthen believers' faith so that they are thoroughly equipped to share His message of love and forgiveness. We begin the sharing at home and move to more distant places, presenting the Gospel as revealed in Scripture.

4. God desires to be active in our lives every day. The Holy Spirit remains active in our lives as we find time to study, read, and meditate on His Word.

Catechism Connection

1. God rules over the whole universe (kingdom of power), the church on earth (kingdom of grace), and the church and angels in heaven (kingdom of glory).

2. God relies on us to spread His kingdom of grace by words and actions.

3. God assures us that His Word will not return empty. We speak the message, but God turns the hearts to faith in Him.

Send

To Do This Week

Urge participants to complete one or more of the suggested activities before the class meets again. Then close with prayer.

For Next Week

Urge participants to read Matthew 3:1–12 and Luke 1:57–80 in preparation for the next session.